JAVASCRIPT

in easy steps

MIKE MCGRATH

In easy steps is an imprint of Computer Step
Southfield Road . Southam
Warwickshire CV47 OFB . England

http://www.ineasysteps.com

Notice of Liability
Every effort has been made to ensure that this book contains accurate
and current information. However, Computer Step and the author shall
not be liable for any loss or damage suffered by readers as a result of
any information contained herein.

Trademarks
All trademarks are acknowledged as belonging to their respective
companies.

Printed and bound in the United Kingdom

ISBN 1-874029-89-X

Table Of Contents

Date and Time 53

5

Doing Mathematics 65

6

Working With Strings 75

7

Addressing Page Objects 87

8

9 Window Properties 97

10 Document Properties 111

11 Form Properties 123

Introducing JavaScript

Welcome to the world of JavaScript. This chapter introduces the JavaScript language and illustrates how to define a JavaScript section inside an HTML document. The JavaScript language keywords are all listed and the essentials of functions and variables are explained.

Covers

Chapter One

Introduction

JavaScript is an interpreted programming language whose interpreter is embedded inside web browser software, such as Microsoft Internet Explorer and Netscape Navigator.

The JavaScript interpreter is an integral part of the browser software so scripts are parsed without delay.

This means that script contained in web documents can be read by the browser's "JavaScript engine" whenever the document is loaded into the browser window.

In this way, web documents can be made to respond to the user's actions and to perform dynamic visual effects.

JavaScript should not be confused with the compiled programming language called Java from Sun Microsystems which, although bearing some resemblance, is a completely different language.

JavaScript appeared in December 1995 and was initially called LiveScript, although the name was soon changed for marketing reasons.

The JavaScript language contains many impressive features but for security reasons it cannot read or write files, with the exception of "cookie" files that store a small amount of data.

This book is concerned with the core and client-side features of JavaScript that are most useful in the creation of interactive web pages.

It is important to learn the basics - so the mechanics of the language are covered first in chapters that explain, by example, how to write JavaScript programs.

Then the browser "document object model" (DOM) is introduced to illustrate how all web pages contain objects with properties that can be manipulated by JavaScript.

Combining JavaScript with knowledge of the DOM enables the powerful creation of dynamic HTML (DHTML) effects.

The final part of this book contains examples of JavaScript in use to create popular DHTML effects, together with full source code that can be used on any web page.

The Script Block

In order to include JavaScript in a web document a script block must first be defined within the HTML code.

The script block can be defined anywhere within the HTML code although the usual place is inside the head section of the document, between the <HEAD> and </HEAD> tags.

When a browser loads a document it reads, or "parses", the code sequentially. So placing the script block in the head of the document ensures that the JavaScript code is parsed before the rest of the HTML and document content.

A script block looks like this :

The LANGUAGE attribute, which was formerly used to specify the scripting language, is deprecated in HTML 4.0 so the TYPE attribute should now be used for this purpose.

```
<SCRIPT TYPE = "text/javascript">

<!--



//-->

</SCRIPT>
```

The actual code will be added between the lines beginning with <!-- and //-->.

These lines are there to hide the script from really old browsers that do not have a JavaScript interpreter.

Javascript code may be separated from the HTML code by writing all the JavaScript code inside a JavaScript file. This is simply a text document, that is saved with a ".js" file extension, and contains no HTML tags whatsoever.

The script reference should still be placed in the document head section with an added SRC attribute pointing the browser to the url of the JavaScript file like this example:

Notice that the </SCRIPT> closing tag is still required.

```
<SCRIPT TYPE= "text/javascript" SRC= "mycode.js">

</SCRIPT>
```

Hello World

To make a JavaScript alert dialog box appear is a simple matter of calling the JavaScript alert() function in the code contained in the script block, like the example below:

```
<SCRIPT TYPE = "text/javascript">

<!--

alert( "Hello World" );

//-->

</SCRIPT>
```

When this document is loaded into the web browser the JavaScript engine implements the instructions contained in the JavaScript code.

In this case, the JavaScript code causes the browser to open an alert dialog box bearing the message contained within the quotation marks inside the brackets.

The title bar in the alert may contain a different title but this is not controlled by JavaScript.

[JavaScript Application]

Hello World

OK

The quotation marks inside the brackets do not actually appear as part of the message because they are just used by JavaScript to denote a string of characters that is the text content of the message itself.

All strings in JavaScript are contained in this way.

Syntax Rules

Notice that there is a semi-colon at the end of the JavaScript statement on the facing page to comply with the required JavaScript language syntax rules.

This must be used at the end of every Javascript statement in the same way that a period is used to terminate a sentence in the English language syntax rules.

Most importantly, JavaScript is a case-sensitive language where "ALERT", "Alert" and "alert" are seen as three different words.

Problems with case can be avoided by using only lowercase throughout JavaScript code.

All JavaScript keywords are in lowercase only so using ALERT("Hello World") or Alert("Hello World") in the facing code would not call the JavaScript alert() function.

Spaces, tabs and new lines are collectively known as whitespace and are completely ignored by JavaScript so the code may be formatted and indented to make its appearance more easily human-readable.

It is often useful to add comments to JavaScript code as explanation. The parser sees any text between // and the end of that line as a single-line comment, which it ignores. Also any text, on one or more lines, between /* and */ is ignored.

```
<SCRIPT TYPE = "text/javascript">

<!--

/* Here is an introduction
to this script code that
uses a multi-line comment */

alert( "Hello World" );

// Here is a single-line comment

//-->

</SCRIPT>
```

Keywords

The following table contains the keywords that are part of the JavaScript language syntax so they may not be used when choosing identifier names for variables, functions or labels:

JavaScript keywords must always appear in lower case.

break	do	function	null	typeof
case	else	if	return	var
continue	export	import	switch	void
default	false	in	this	while
delete	for	new	true	with

Additionally, JavaScript reserves all the words listed in the table below for possible future inclusion into the JavaScript syntax – so these too may not be used as identifier names. Although this may seem to be a lot of words to avoid it is seldom a real problem – it's just a point to remember.

abstract	debugger	goto	package	synchronized
boolean	double	implements	private	throw
byte	enum	instanceof	protected	throws
catch	extends	int	public	transient
char	final	interface	short	try
class	finally	long	static	
const	float	native	super	

Variables

A variable is a place in which to store data for manipulation within a JavaScript program.

When naming variables any letter, digit and the underscore character "_" may be used but the variable name may not begin with a digit. These are all valid variable names:

```
abc

my_first_variable

var123
```

Create a new variable using the JavaScript "var" keyword:

```
<SCRIPT TYPE = "text/javascript">

<!--

var message = "First JavaScript Variable";

alert( message );

//-->

</SCRIPT>
```

The text string is stored inside the variable named message.

The variable name is used in the call to the JavaScript alert function that opens an alert dialog box displaying the string that is stored in the variable.

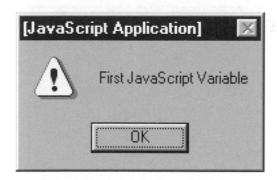

Data Types

JavaScript is a loosely typed language so its variables can store numbers, text strings or boolean values (true / false).

This is unlike other programming languages such as C++ and Java that need to declare variables of a specific data type and can only then store data of the declared type.

Notice that JavaScript makes no distinction between integer numbers and floating-point numbers.

```
<SCRIPT TYPE = "text/javascript">

<!--

var a = 0.06;

var b = "JavaScript in easy steps";

var c = false;

alert( typeof a + "\n" + typeof b + "\n" + typeof c );

//-->

</SCRIPT>
```

The example above creates variables with initial values of the three different data types supported by JavaScript.

These three values are first passed to the alert() function, then the JavaScript keyword typeof is used to return their data types for display in the alert dialog box shown below.

The code "+\n+" inside the brackets just displays the output for each value on a new line in the alert dialog box.

Escape Sequences

When a character in a string is preceded by the backslash character "\" there is a special effect on the character immediately following the backslash. This is known as an escape sequence as it allows the character to escape recognition as part of the JavaScript syntax.

The table below lists more escape sequences:

The code example on the facing page uses the "\n" newline escape.

\b	Backspace
\f	Formfeed
\n	New line
\r	Carriage return
\t	Tab
\'	Single quote that will not terminate a string
\"	Double quote that will not terminate a string
\\	Single backslash character

The escape sequence " \" " is useful to incorporate quotation marks within a string without the string itself becoming terminated, as in this example:

```
alert( "We all say \"JavaScript is great\" " );
```

Functions

A function is a piece of Javascript code that can be executed once or many times by the JavaScript application. Functions and variables form the basis of all JavaScript programming.

This is how a function looks:

Always try to give meaningful names to functions and variables, describing their purpose.

```
function call_alert(){

alert( "My First JavaScript Function" );

}
```

Create a new function using the JavaScript "function" keyword followed by a given identifier name. The name must be unique within the script and adhere to the same naming conventions that apply to the naming of variables.

The name is always followed by a pair of plain brackets then a pair of curly brackets containing the code to be executed.

In the example the function has been named call_alert() and the code to be executed will call the JavaScript alert() function to display an alert dialog box containing a message.

The function can be called from anywhere in the document to execute the statement that it contains.

The "onload" attribute of the HTML body tag can call the function when the document is loaded as in this example:

Remember to include the plain brackets when referring to a function.

```
<BODY ONLOAD = "call_alert()">
```

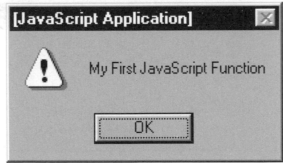

Function Arguments

The plain brackets that follow the name of all functions may be used to contain data for use in the code to be executed. Just as the brackets of the JavaScript alert() function contain the string to be displayed in the alert dialog box it creates.

The data contained within the brackets is known as the function "argument".

In the example below the function call passes a string to the argument named "str" in the call_alert() function for use in the code that is to be executed.

"str" is often used in JavaScripts as a variable name for strings.

```
function call_alert( str ){

alert( str );

}
```

```
<BODY ONLOAD = "call_alert( 'Passed Value' )">
```

It is important to note that string contained inside the call is enclosed in single quotes to differentiate it from the double quotes used to contain the entire call.

Using double quotes for both would mean that the onload attribute value would be "call_alert(" because the string is terminated by the second double quote. This would create a browser error and the function would not be executed.

The use of single and double quotes in this manner appears throughout JavaScript programming in several ways.

Multiple Functions

JavaScript functions may call other functions during the execution of their code in just the same way that the previous examples called the JavaScript alert() function.

The following example demonstrates the use of multiple functions to manipulate and display an integer argument:

The plus sign is used both to concatenate text when used with strings and to perform addition when used with numbers.

```
function call_alert( num ){

var new_number = make_double( num );

alert( "The Value Is " + new_number );

}

function make_double( num ){

var double_num = num + num;

return double_num;

}
```

```
<BODY ONLOAD = "call_alert( 4 )">
```

The argument value is passed from the caller to the make_double() function via the call_alert() function.

The value is manipulated by the code in the function body and the result is returned to a new variable in the call_alert() function using the JavaScript "return" keyword. Finally the alert() function is called to display the variable value.

Variable Scope

The variables used in the example on the facing page are both declared inside a function so they are called "local" variables. Local variables can only be used by the function in which they are declared.

Conversely, "global" variables are declared outside functions and can be accessed by any function in the same document.

All variables may simply be declared without being "initialized" with an initial value.

```
var stored_num;

function call_alert( num ){

stored_num = num;

make_triple();

alert( "The Value Is " + stored_num );

}

function make_triple(){

stored_num= stored_num + stored_num + stored_num;

}
```

```
<BODY ONLOAD = "call_alert( 5 )">
```

This example passes the argument value to a global variable.

The second function manipulates the value of the global variable before calling alert() to display the new value.

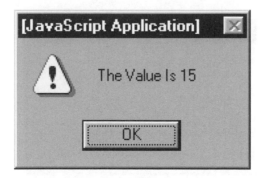

Multiple Arguments

JavaScript functions may contain multiple arguments if they are separated by a comma.

The number of arguments defined when the function is declared must be exactly matched by the number of arguments contained in any call to that function.

This example declares a function containing three arguments so any call to it must contain three argument values:

The var keyword can be used to declare multiple variables by separating the variable names with a comma.

```
var a, b, c;

function call_alert( str1, str2, str3 ){

a = str1;

b = str2;

c = str3;

alert( a + b + c );

}
```

```
<BODY ONLOAD = "call_alert( 'Great',' ','JavaScript' )">
```

The caller passes three strings to the function although the value of the second string is merely a space.

The function assigns the argument values to three global variables and then calls alert() to display the global values as a single concatenated string.

Performing Operations

All the common JavaScript operators are detailed in this chapter which illustrates by example how to perform arithmetical operations, how to assign values and how to make comparisons. The logical operators are explained and demonstrated too, along with the conditional operator.

Covers

Chapter Two

Arithmetical Operators

The arithmetical operators commonly used in JavaScript are listed in the table below with the operations they perform:

Operator	Operation
+	Addition (and concatenates strings)
-	Subtraction
*	Multiplication
/	Division
%	Modulo
++	Increment
- -	Decrement

Notice that the "+" operator has two types of operation depending on the given operands. It will add together two numeric values and give the result of the addition. It will also join together two string values and return the concatenated string, as in the example on the facing page.

An example using the modulo operator to determine odd or even values can be found in the if statement example on page 32.

The modulo operator will divide the first given number by the second given number and return the remainder of the operation. This is most useful to determine if a number has an odd or even value.

The increment ++ and decrement -- operators alter the given value by 1 and return the resulting new value. These are most commonly used to count iterations in a loop.

All the other operators act as you would expect but care should be taken to bracket expressions where more than one operator is being used to clarify the operations:

```
a = b * c - d % e / f ;          \\ This is unclear

a = (b * c) - ((d % e) / f );    \\ This is clear
```

Arithmetical Examples

```
var addnum = 20 + 30;

var addstr = "I love " + "JavaScript";

var sub = 35.75 - 28.25;

var mul = 8 * 50;

var mod =  65 % 2;

var inc = 5 ; inc = ++inc;

var dec = 5 ; dec = --dec;

var result = "Addnum is " + addnum + "\n";

result += "Addstr is " + addstr + "\n";

result += "Sub is " + sub + "\n";

result += "Mul is " + mul + "\n";

result += "Mod is " + mod + "\n";

result += "Inc is " + inc + "\n";

result += "Dec is " + dec + "\n";

alert ( result );
```

The increment and decrement operators may also be used following the operand. Note that in those cases they will perform the operation but only return the unoperated value.

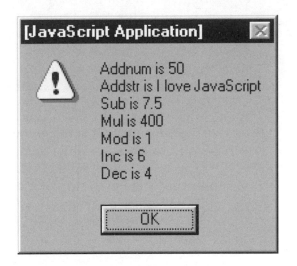

```
[JavaScript Application]

    Addnum is 50
    Addstr is I love JavaScript
    Sub is 7.5
    Mul is 400
    Mod is 1
    Inc is 6
    Dec is 4

            OK
```

Logical Operators

The three logical operators that can be used in JavaScript are listed in the table below:

Operator	Operation
&&	Logical AND
||	Logical OR
!	Logical NOT

The logical operators are used with operands that have the boolean values of true or false, or are values that can convert to true or false.

There is an example of conditional branching in the conditional operator demo on page 30.

The logical "&&" operator will evaluate two operands and return true only if both operands themselves are true. Otherwise the "&&" operator will return false.

This is typically used in "conditional branching" where the direction of a JavaScript application is determined by testing two conditions. If both conditions are satisfied the script will go in a certain direction otherwise the script will take a different direction.

Unlike the "&&" operator that needs both operands to be true the "||" operator will evaluate its two operands and return true if either one of the operands itself returns true. If neither operand returns true then "||" will return false. This is useful in a JavaScript application to perform a certain action if either one of two test conditions has been met.

An example using the ! operator as a toggle can be found in the loop demo on page 39.

The third logical operator "!" is a unary operator that is used before a single operand. It returns the inverse value of the given operand so if the variable "a" had a value of true then "!a" would have a value of false. It is useful in JavaScript applications to toggle the value of a variable in successive loop iterations with a statement like "a=!a". This will ensure that on each pass the value is changed, like flicking a light switch on and off.

Logical Examples

```
var a =  true , b = false;

var test1 = ( a && a );  // test both operands for true

var test2 = ( a && b );

var test3 = ( b && b );

var test4 = ( a || b );  // test either operand for true

var test5 = ( a || b );

var test6 = ( b || b );

var test7 = !a ; var test8 = !b;    // invert values

var result = "AND \n";

result += "1: " +test1+ "    2: " +test2+ "    3: "+test3;

result += "\n\nOR\n";

result += "4: "+test4+"   5: "+test5+"   6: "+test6;

result += "\n\n!\n7: " +test7+ "    8: " + test8;

alert( result );
```

Use the "\n" new line escape, and spaces to format the displayed output string.

Assignment Operators

The operators that are commonly used in JavaScript to assign values are all listed in the table below. All except the simple assign operator "=" are a shorthand form of a longer expression so each equivalent is also given for clarity.

Operator	Example	Equivalent
=	a = b	a = b
+=	a += b	a = a + b
-=	a -= b	a = a - b
*=	a *= b	a = a * b
/=	a /= b	a = a / b
%=	a %= b	a = a % b

The equality operator compares values and is explained fully, with examples, on page 28.

It is important to regard the "=" operator to mean "assign" rather than "equals" to avoid confusion with the equality operator "==".

In the example in the table the variable named "a" is assigned the value that is contained in the variable named "b" to become its new value.

The "+=" operator is most useful and has been used in earlier examples to add a second string to an existing string. In the table example the "+=" operator adds the value contained in variable "a" to the value contained in the variable named "b" then assigns the result to become the new value contained in variable "a".

All other operators in the table work in the same way by making the arithmetical operation between the two values first, then assigning the result to the first variable to become its new value.

Assignment Examples

```javascript
var a= "JavaScript", b= " Code"; // assign string values

a += b;               // concatenate strings and assign to a

var c= 8, d= 4;               // assign integer values

c += d;               // add numbers and assign result to c

var e= 7.5, f= 2.25;               // assign float values

e -= f;        // subtract f from e and assign result to e

var g= 8, h= 4;               // assign integer values

g *= h;        // multiply numbers and assign result to g

var i= 8, j= 4;               // assign integer values

i /= j;          // divide i by j and assign result to i

var k= 8, l= 4;               // assign integer values

k %= l;        // divide k by l and assign remainder to k
```

The results are displayed using the alert() function, as before, but that part of the code has been omitted to save space.

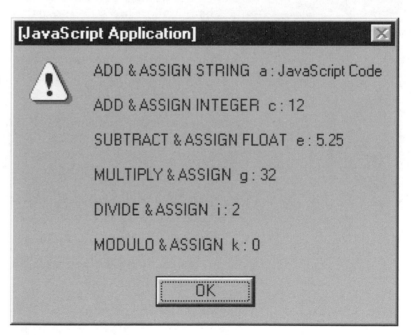

Comparison Operators

The operators that are commonly used in JavaScript to compare two values are all listed in the table below:

Operator	Comparative Test
==	Equality
!=	Inequality
>	Greater than
<	Less than
>=	Greater than or equal to
<=	Less than or equal to

An example of the "less than" operator "<" in a JavaScript loop statement can be found on page 36.

The equality operator "==" compares two operands and will return true if both are equal in value. If both are the same number they are equal, or if both are strings containing the same characters in the same positions they are equal. Boolean operands that are both true, or both false, are equal.

Conversely the "!=" operator returns true if two operands are not equal using the same rules as the "==" operator.

Equality and inequality operators are useful in testing the state of two variables to perform conditional branching.

"Greater than" operators compares two operands and will return true if the first is greater in value than the second.

"Less than" operators makes the same comparison but return true if the first operand is less in value than the second.

Adding the "=" operator after a "greater than" or "less than" operator makes it also return true if the two operands are exactly equal in value.

The "greater than" operator ">" is frequently used to test the value of a countdown value in a loop.

Comparison Examples

Notice that the capitalization should also match to make strings equal.

```javascript
var teststrings1 = ( "JavaScript" == "JavaScript" );

var teststrings2 = ( "JavaScript" == "javascript" );

var testnumbers1 = ( 1.785 == 1.785 );

var testnumbers2 = ( 5 != 5 );

var testbooleans1 = ( true == true );

var testbooleans2 = ( false != false );

var testlessthan1 = ( 100 < 200 );

var testlessthan2 = ( 100 < 100 );

var testlessthan_or_equal = ( 100 <= 100 );

var testgreaterthan = ( -1 > 1 );

var a = 8, b = 8.0, testvariables1 = ( a == b );

var c = null, d = null, testvariables2 = ( c == d );
```

null is a JavaScript keyword meaning there is no value.

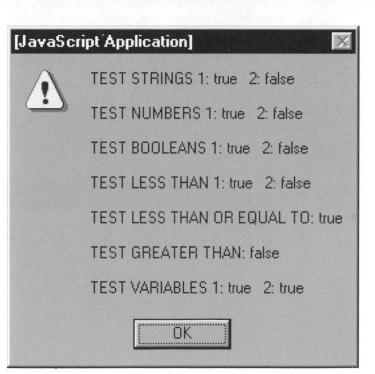

```
[JavaScript Application]                    X

 !    TEST STRINGS 1: true   2: false

      TEST NUMBERS 1: true   2: false

      TEST BOOLEANS 1: true   2: false

      TEST LESS THAN 1: true   2: false

      TEST LESS THAN OR EQUAL TO: true

      TEST GREATER THAN: false

      TEST VARIABLES 1: true   2: true

                  [    OK    ]
```

Conditional Operator

The JavaScript coder's favourite comparison operator is probably the conditional operator. This first evaluates an expression for a true or false value then executes one of two given statements depending on the result of the evaluation.

The conditional operator has this syntax:

```
(test expression) ? if true do this : if false do this;
```

This operator can often be used to run script functions that are dedicated to a particular web browser following a browser-identification routine. The example below is to display a welcome message determined by browser type:

A full example with browser identification can be found on page 93.

```
var browser= browserID; // Internet Explorer or Netscape

( browser == "IE" ) ? greetIEuser() : greetNNuser();
```

Making Statements

Statements are used in JavaScript to progress the execution of the JavaScript application. They may define loops within the code or be simple terms to be evaluated. This chapter examines conditional testing and the different types of loops with examples of their use.

Covers

Chapter Three

Conditional If

The "if" keyword is used to perform the basic conditional JavaScript test to evaluate an expression for a boolean value. The statement following the evaluation will only be executed when the expression returns true. The syntax for the "if" statement looks like this:

```
if ( test expression ) statement to execute when true ;
```

The code to be executed may contain multiple statements if they are enclosed within a pair of curly braces to form a "statement block".

In the example below the expression to be tested uses the modulo operator to determine if the value contained in the variable called "num" is exactly divisible by 2. The statement block has two statements - one to assign a string value to a variable and another to call a JavaScript function.

The expression could have used (num%2==1) to detect an odd number.

```
var msg, num;

num = 7;

if ( num % 2 != 0 ) {

msg = "This is an odd number.";

alert( msg );

}
```

If - Prompt Example

This example calls the JavaScript prompt() function which needs two arguments to be supplied by the caller. The first argument is the message to be displayed and the second is a default entry in the input field, in this case an empty string.

The user input is assigned to the "username" variable and is displayed by the alert function if the string is not still empty.

```
var username = null;

if ( username == null ){

username = prompt( "Please Enter Your Name", "" );

if ( username != "" ) alert( "Welcome " + username );

}
```

The prompt dialog will open with an empty input field but is shown here following user input.

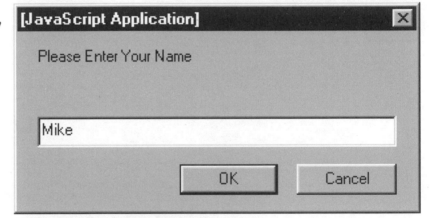

If-Else Statements

The JavaScript "else" keyword can be used with an "if" statement to provide alternative code to execute in the event that the test expression returns false.

This is known as "conditional branching" and has this syntax:

```
if (test expression ) do this; else do this;
```

Several expressions may be tested until a true value is found when the code following the true expression will be executed. It is important to note any further code contained in the "if-else" statement is ignored.

So in the following example any code after the call to the alert function by the third test will be ignored completely:

```
var num = 2, bool = false;

if(num== 1 && bool== 1)  alert("TEST1 bool: "+bool);

else

if(num== 2 && bool== 1)  alert("TEST2 bool: "+bool);

else

if(num== 2 && bool== 0)  alert("TEST3 bool: "+bool);

else

if(num== 3 && bool== 0)  alert("TEST4 bool: "+bool);
```

The Switch Statement

Conditional branching using the "if-else" statement may be more efficiently performed using a "switch" statement when a test expression evaluates the value of just one variable.

The switch statement works in an unusual way. First it evaluates a given expression then seeks a label to match the resulting value. The code associated with the matching label will be executed or, if no match is made, the statement will execute any specified default code.

The JavaScript "case" keyword is used to denote a label and the "default" keyword denotes the default code.

For more detail on the break statement see page 40.

All label code must be terminated by a break statement using the JavaScript "break" keyword.

The labels may be numbers, strings, or booleans but must all be of the same type like this example using number types:

Omitting the ending break keywords will allow execution of all other code in the switch statement.

```
var num= 2;

switch(num){

case 1 : alert("This is case 1 code"); break;

case 2 : alert("This is case 2 code"); break;

case 3 : alert("This is case 3 code"); break;

default : alert("This is default code");

}
```

For Loops

The "for" loop is probably the most frequently used type of loop in JavaScript and has this syntax:

```
for ( initializer , test , increment ) statement ;
```

The initializer is used to set the start value for the counter of the number of loop iterations. A variable may be declared here for this purpose and it is traditional to name it "i".

At each pass of the loop a boolean condition is tested and the next iteration of the loop will only run if the condition returns true. If the test returns false then the loop will end.

With every iteration the counter is incremented then the loop will execute the code in the statement. Multiple statements can be executed if they are contained by curly braces in a statement block.

The following example makes five iterations and changes the assigned value of two variables at each pass:

A "for" loop can count down - decrementing the counter at each iteration.

```
var a = 0, b = 0;

for ( var i = 0; i < 5; i++ ){

a += 10; b += 5;

}

alert( "FOR LOOP\n\n A is " + a + "... B is " + b );
```

The For-In Loop

The "for-in" loop has a special use to enumerate all the variables or properties contained within an object.

This loop is seldom used in regular JavaScript but is included here because it can reveal the properties available for manipulation within a web browser.

The following example reveals a tantalising glimpse of the properties available within the window object of the Microsoft Internet Explorer 5.0 web browser:

The properties revealed will vary for each browser and version.

```
var i = 0 ; a = "";

for ( property in window ){

a += property + "...";

}

alert( a );
```

The properties revealed with this script are part of the document object model (DOM) that is detailed in chapter 8.

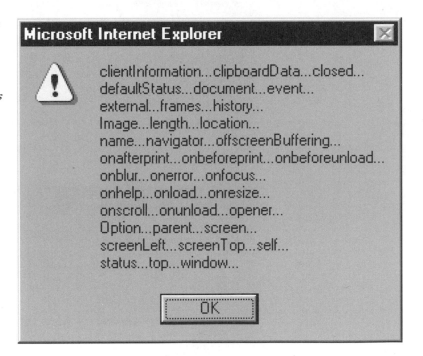

Microsoft Internet Explorer

clientInformation...clipboardData...closed...
defaultStatus...document...event...
external...frames...history...
Image...length...location...
name...navigator...offscreenBuffering...
onafterprint...onbeforeprint...onbeforeunload...
onblur...onerror...onfocus...
onhelp...onload...onresize...
onscroll...onunload...opener...
Option...parent...screen...
screenLeft...screenTop...self...
status...top...window...

OK

While Loops

Another loop uses the JavaScript "while" keyword followed by an expression to be evaluated for a boolean value.

If the evaluation returns true then the code in the statement block will be executed. After the code has executed the test expression will again be evaluated and the loop will continue until the evaluation returns false.

An infinite loop will lock the script and crash the browser.

The statement block must feature code that will affect the test expression in order to change the evaluation result to return false otherwise an infinite loop will be created.

It is important to note that if the test expression returns false when it is first evaluated then the code in the statement block is never executed.

This example decrements a variable value on each iteration of the loop and the counter increments until it reaches 10 when the evaluation returns false and the loop ends.

```
var i= 0, num= 50;

while( i < 10 ){

num--;

i++;

}

alert( "Loop stopped at " + i + "\nnum is now " + num );
```

The Do-While Loop

The JavaScript "do" keyword is used to denote the start of a "do-while loop" and is followed by a statement block containing the code to be executed by the loop.

The statement code is followed by the JavaScript "while" keyword and an expression to be evaluated for a boolean value of true or false.

If the evaluation returns true the loop restarts at the "do" keyword and will continue until the evaluation returns false.

It is important to note that , unlike the simple "while" loop, the statement code will always be executed at least once by the "do-while" loop because the test expression is not encountered until the end of the loop.

The following example will never loop because the counter value is incremented to 1 in the first execution of the statement code so the first test evaluation will return false:

A while loop is often more suitable than a do-while loop.

```
var i= 0, num= 50;

do{

num--;

i++;

}while( i < 1 );

alert( "Loop stopped at " + i + "\nnum is now " + num );
```

Break Statement

The JavaScript "break" keyword is used to terminate the execution of a loop prematurely.

The "break" keyword is situated inside the statement block containing the code that the loop should execute and is preceded by a conditional test.

When the test condition is met the "break" statement immediately terminates the loop and no further iterations are made.

Notice in the alert output below that the counter value is still three because the increment in the final iteration is not applied

In the following example the conditional test will return true when the counter value reaches three:

```
var i= 0;

while( i < 6 ){

if( i == 3 ) break;

i++;

}

alert( "BREAK\n\nLoop stopped at " + i );
```

The "break" keyword is also used as a terminator when used with a "switch" statement.

Continue Statement

The JavaScript "continue" keyword is used to break the current iteration of a loop.

Just like the "break" keyword the "continue" keyword is situated inside the statement block containing the code that the loop should execute, preceded by a conditional test.

When the test condition is met the "continue" keyword immediately stops the current iteration of the loop but further iterations will be made until the loop ends.

In the example below the test condition is met when the counter value reaches three so the string concatenation in that iteration is not applied but the loop continues on.

The loop counter should be incremented before the "continue" condition is tested to avoid creating an infinite loop.

```
var i= 0, str= "";

while( i < 5 ){

i++;

if( i == 3 )continue;

str += i + " ";

}

alert("CONTINUE\n\nLoop stopped:"+i+"\n\nSeries:"+str );
```

Using With Statements

The JavaScript "with" keyword is used to reference object properties without needing to add the object name before each property name.

This is most useful when writing JavaScript applications to produce dynamic effects as these scripts often refer to document objects.

See Chapter 10 for more about document objects and properties.

For example, every web page contains a "document" object that in turn has a "forms" property to reference forms on the web page. Elements of the form may have their values set by JavaScript as in this example:

```
document.forms.order.user.value = "Mike";

document.forms.order.city.value = "London";
```

These assignments can be expressed more clearly using a "with" statement like this:

```
with( document.forms.order ){

user.value = "Mike";

city.value = "London";

}
```

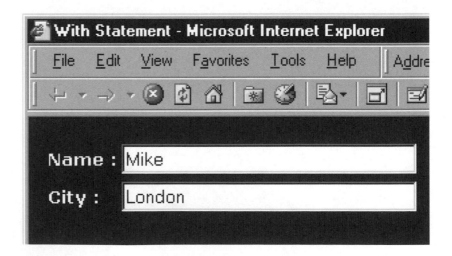

Using Arrays

This chapter deals exclusively with the topic of arrays and illustrates by example what they are and how to use them. The examples include a practical use of arrays to preload images into a web browser.

Covers

Chapter Four

Creating Arrays

An array is like a variable that can contain multiple values, unlike a regular variable that may only contain a single value.

A variable is given array status using the JavaScript "new" keyword along with the JavaScript "Array()" constructor.

Multiple data values can then be assigned to the array using the array name together with an index number, starting at zero, placed inside square brackets like in this example:

```
var a = new Array();

a[0] = "First";

a[1] = "JavaScript";

a[2] = "Array";
```

The array values can now be used just like regular variables.

For small arrays it is often more convenient to initialize the array values as arguments in the Array() constructor as illustrated in this example which uses three arrays:

Remember that an array index starts at zero. So a[2] is the third element in the index, not the second.

```
var a = new Array("21st ", "22nd ", "23rd ");

var b = new Array("Jan,", "Feb,", "Mar,");

var c = new Array(" 2001", " 2002", " 2003");

alert( a[0] + b[1] + c[2] );
```

Array Elements

Each value held in an array is called an array "element".

Find more on properties, objects and constructors at pages 88/89.

When a variable is given array status using the "new Array()" constructor it also gets properties and methods that can be used to manipulate the elements contained in the array.

One of the most useful of these is the "length" property that may be used to report the number of elements that the array currently contains.

The syntax to use a property or method just tacks a period and the name onto the object. So "array.length" references the length property of the array object.

Notice that an array containing three values will have a length of 3, but because indexing starts at zero the last element in the array will have an index number of only 2.

The example below demonstrates this point:

Optionally the Array() constructor may take an argument to specify the number of array elements to create, such as var a = new Array(8);

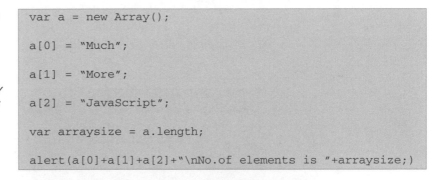

```
var a = new Array();

a[0] = "Much";

a[1] = "More";

a[2] = "JavaScript";

var arraysize = a.length;

alert(a[0]+a[1]+a[2]+"\nNo.of elements is "+arraysize;)
```

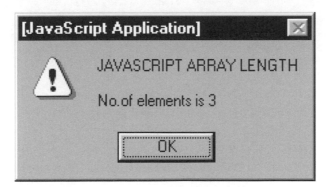

Fill Elements Loop

All types of loops can be used to easily fill the elements of an array with a large number of data values. This is the major attraction of arrays and it is achieved with very little code.

The example below first creates an array then, on each iteration, the "for" loop fills each of the array elements with a string value to which is added the current counter value.

Each element value is concatenated in the "str" variable before finally displaying in the alert dialog box:

This code could be used to fill 100 elements just by making the conditional value of 8 into 100.

```
var str = "FILL ELEMENTS LOOP\n\n";

var arr = new Array();

for( var i = 0; i < 8; i++ ){

arr[ i ] = "Number is " + i + "\n";

str += arr[ i ];

}

alert( str );
```

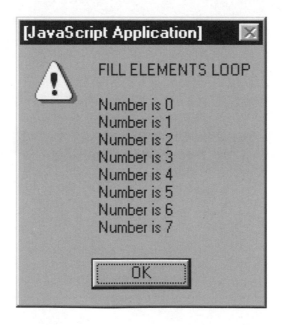

Adding More Elements

Additional elements can be added to an array, without specifying an actual index number, by using the array.length property to find the next available empty element.

Because the array.length value exceeds the last index number by one it will always specify the next free element when it is used as the index number between square brackets.

The example below illustrates this when assigning the integer 4 to the next free element in the "a" array.

The "b" array elements are initialized, then the "for" loop successively assigns the "b" array element values to each free element in the "a" array.

Finally all "a" array elements are displayed by the alert() function in concatenated form by the array.concat() method.

The method array.concat() will display all the element values in an array, separated by commas.

```
var a = new Array( 1, 2, 3 );

a[ a.length ] = 4;              // a.length is 3

var b = new Array( 5, 6, 7 );

for(var i = 0; i < b.length; i++ ){

a[a.length] = b[i];

}

alert( a.concat() );
```

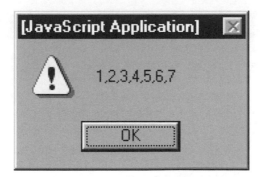

String Of Elements

The JavaScript array.join() method will convert all array elements to strings and concatenate them.

Used without arguments this will return a list of all the array element values separated by commas, like the array.concat() method on the previous page.

But the array.join() method can accept an optional argument to specify an alternative separator to the default comma separator.

Most usefully this can be a space so that result of the array.join() method will be a single string with space separators, as illustrated in the example below:

Escape the single quotes with a "\n" backslash to avoid errors.

```
var a = new Array();

a[0] = "It";

a[1] = "isn\'t";

a[2] = "rocket";

a[3] = "science -";

a[4] = "it\'s";

a[5] = "just";

a[6] = "JavaScript";

alert( a.join(" ") );
```

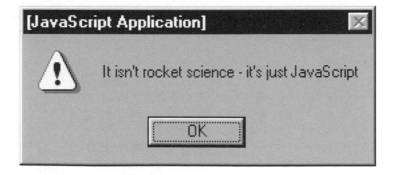

Reverse Element Order

Arrays can be used to contain a file name or complete url in each element for use with dynamic features in web pages.

A complete slide show script is given on page 166.

One such popular use is with JavaScript slide shows that rotate a series of images with a set delay between each one.

An array is used to hold the url of each image in its elements so that the script can easily reference them by array index.

If the slide show is required to reverse after displaying the final image, rather than start over at the first image, this can be achieved by reversing the element order inside the array.

The following example creates an initial array of just three images whose order will be reversed after the final image displays and the rev variable is set to true:

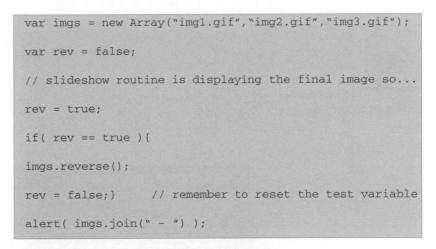

```
var imgs = new Array("img1.gif","img2.gif","img3.gif");

var rev = false;

// slideshow routine is displaying the final image so...

rev = true;

if( rev == true ){

imgs.reverse();

rev = false;}       // remember to reset the test variable

alert( imgs.join(" - ") );
```

The evaluation (rev == true) can be abbreviated to a simple (rev).

[JavaScript Application]

img3.gif - img2.gif - img1.gif

OK

Subarrays

The JavaScript array.slice() method is useful to make a new array from an existing array using some of the existing element values.

This method takes two arguments to specify the index numbers of elements in the original array where the new array elements should start and end.

The second argument may have a negative value to indicate the element position from the end of the array.

If only a single argument is specified it will be used as the first element index number and the method will return a new array with all elements from this position onwards.

These examples illustrate the different ways in which the array.slice() method can be used:

The array elements are taken up to, but not including, the second argument index.

```
var a = new Array( 1, 2, 3, 4, 5, 6, 7, 8 );

var b = a.slice( 2, 5 );

var c = a.slice( 1, -1 );

var d = a.slice( 3 );
```

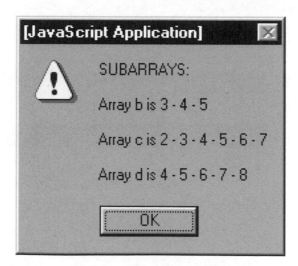

Arrange Elements

The JavaScript array.sort() method allows string element values to be arranged in alphabetic order.

This is sometimes desirable so that the output can be presented alphabetically.

Integer and floating point numeric values will be arranged in ascending order as seen in the following example:

Negative numeric values are arranged as -1,-2,-3, etc.

```javascript
var integers = new Array( 3, 8, 1, 9, 7, 5, 4, 2, 6 );
integers.sort();

var floats = new Array( 0.5, 0.125, 0.75, 0.25 );
floats.sort();

var strings = new Array( "Michael", "Andrew", "David" );
strings.sort();

var str = "SORT";

str += "\n\nIntegers array is " + integers.join(" - ");

str += "\n\nFloats array is " + floats.join(" - ");

str += "\n\nStrings array is " + strings.join(" - ");

alert( str );
```

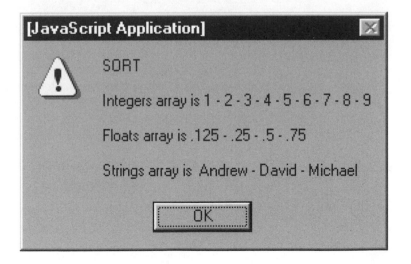

Preloader Array

Rollover images in web pages use a JavaScript effect to swap the original image for a replacement when the user places the cursor over the image.

In order for this effect to work smoothly, without download delay, the required replacement image must be already loaded into the browser cache.

The way to do this is to use a JavaScript preload routine that forces the browser to download the image by creating new Image() objects that use the swap images as their source.

A preload array is used with the slide show script example on page 166.

```
<SCRIPT TYPE="text/javascript">

<!--

var pics = new Array("pic1.gif","pic2.gif","pic3.gif");

var preload = new Array();

for(var i = 0; i < pics.length; i++ ){

preload[ i ] = new Image();

preload[ i ].src = pics[ i ];

}

//-->

</SCRIPT>
```

The script example above uses arrays to preload three swap images to be ready when the rollover effect is activated.

The first array contains the url of each image file.

For each element in the "pics" array the "for" loop creates a corresponding element in the preload array.

Each of the preload elements is made into an Image() object, then the image urls are assigned to their src property so that the browser will download the image files.

Date and Time

This chapter describes by example how to use date and time information in JavaScript. The Date object and the Universal Time Clock are explained along with the JavaScript timer routine. There is also a full script example of a JavaScript clock.

Covers

Chapter Five

Getting Date & Time

Date and time is often used in JavaScripts to customize the performance of a web page. For example, a script might welcome a user with a greeting appropriate to current time:

The script for this application is contained in the example on page 56.

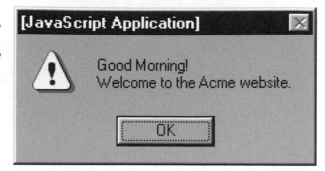

The date and time that is used in JavaScript is taken from the clock and calendar in the host system that is running the browser application in which the script is loaded.

To access the system clock information the script must first create a date object.

This is achieved in the same manner in which an array object is created, using the JavaScript "new" keyword, but now with the JavaScript "Date()" constructor. The example below creates and displays a new date object:

```
var now = new Date();

alert( now );
```

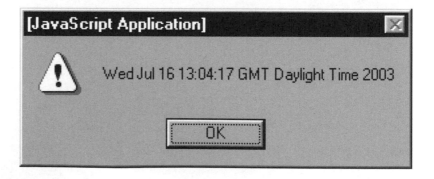

Date Information

The date object has special methods that may be used to retrieve individual parts of the date information.

Some methods return the date information as an index number that often needs to be converted by the script.

The date.getDay() method returns the day of the week as an index value from 0 (Sunday) through to 6 (Saturday).

Month indexing starts at zero so the index in July is 6 not 7.

Also the date.getMonth() method returns the month of the year as an index value from 0 (January) to 11 (December).

The example below illustrates the date methods and uses two arrays to display the correct day and month names:

```
var days = new Array("Sun", "Mon", "Tue", "Wed", "Thu",
"Fri", "Sat");

var mons= new Array("Jan", "Feb", "Mar", "Apr", "May",
"Jun", "Jul", "Aug", "Sep", "Oct", "Nov", "Dec");

var now=new Date();

var yy = now.getYear();

var mm = now.getMonth(); mm=mons[mm];

var dd = now.getDate();

var dy = now.getDay();    dy=days[dy];

alert(dy+" "+dd+" "+mm+" "+yy);
```

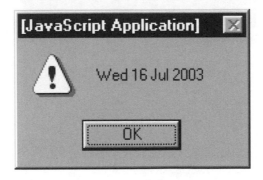

Time Information

The date object has special methods to access the time information that it contains. The example below gets the current hours, minutes, seconds and milliseconds from the host clock and displays a welcome message appropriate for the time of day:

The hours are returned as numbers 0-23 in 24-hour format.

```
var now = new Date();

var hh = now.getHours();

var mn = now.getMinutes();

var ss = now.getSeconds();

var ms = now.getMilliseconds();

var hi = "Good Morning";

if( hh > 11 ) hi= "Good Afternoon";

if( hh > 17 ) hi= "Good Evening";

var tim = hi + "\n";

tim += "Hours: " +hh+ "\n";

tim += "Minutes: " +mn+ "\n";

tim += "Seconds: " +ss+ "." +ms;

alert(tim);
```

Current Time

The JavaScript date.getTime() method can be used to compare two date objects numerically.

The method returns a number that is the difference in milliseconds between the date object value and midnight on the 1st January 1970.

The example below creates a date object both before and after running a loop, then compares the values returned by the date.getTime() method to calculate the time taken to execute the loop.

 If running this example in a Netscape browser reduce the iterations from 250,000 to 5,000.

```
var start = new Date();

var msec1 = start.getTime();

var num = 0;

for( var i = 0; i < 250000; i++ ){

num++;

}

var stop  = new Date();

var msec2 = stop.getTime();

var diff = ( msec2 - msec1 ) / 1000;

alert("Time elapsed: "+diff+ " seconds" );
```

Universal Time Clock

Universal Time is the standard world time clock that runs at Greenwich Mean Time.

The date object methods used in the previous examples all return the local system time but sometimes it is preferable to use the standard of Universal Time.

For this the date object has a series of methods that convert the time and date information from local time to Universal.

The example below calls local and Universal time information on a PC running at Western European Time:

If the minutes are less than 10 the value is a single digit, so this script adds a leading zero to it.

```javascript
var now = new Date();

var hh = now.getHours();

var mn = now.getMinutes();

if( mn <= 9 ) mn = "0" +mn;

var ss = now.getSeconds();

var utc_hh = now.getUTCHours();

var wet = "Athens time: "+hh+": "+mn+": "+ss+"\n\n";

var utc = "Universal time: "+utc_hh+": "+mn+": "+ss;

alert( wet + utc );
```

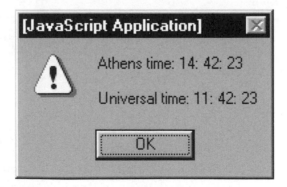

Time Zones

JavaScript can determine which time zone the user is in using the date.getTimezoneOffset() method.

The method gets the local time from the date object then compares it to the UTC time. The return value is the difference stated in minutes because some countries have time zones at other than regular one-hour intervals.

In the example below the date.getTimezoneOffset() method decides in which US timezone, if any, the user is located:

This method can easily be used to redirect users to a local web page too.

```javascript
var now = new Date();

var offset = now.getTimezoneOffset();

var msg;

switch(offset){

case 240 : msg = "East Coast"; break;

case 300 : msg = "Central"; break;

case 360 : msg = "Mountain"; break;

case 420 : msg = "Pacific"; break;

default  : msg = "all";

}

alert("Welcome to " +msg+ " visitors.");
```

A bug in some Netscape browsers does not report the correct offset.

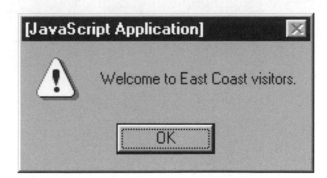

Setting Date And Time

The JavaScript code may manipulate the date object information using a variety of date.set methods.

These mirror the range of date.get methods that are used to extract parts of the date object information but are used instead to set new values.

In the example below the initial date object values are stored in the "orig" variable then the various date.set methods apply new values to the date object information:

The toString() method used here returns the string value of JavaScript objects and has many uses.

```javascript
var now = new Date();

var orig = "Original :\n " +now.toString()+ "\n\n";

now.setDate(21);

now.setMonth(1);

now.setHours(12);

now.setMinutes(30);

now.setSeconds(15);

now.setFullYear(2005);

var mod = "Modified :\n " + now;

alert( orig + mod );
```

Date Strings

In many instances the date object information must be converted into a string in order to store or use that information.

The date.toString() method on the facing page does this but it is often preferable to store this information in standard UTC time.

JavaScript provides the date.toGMTString() method that both converts the information to a string and converts it to the GMT timezone.

A complete example setting cookies using this method can be found in Chapter 10, on page 114.

Using this method of storing date information avoids timezone confusion and is commonly used as the standard when setting the life span of cookie files.

This simple example illustrates the date.toGMTString() method performing its conversions in a browser in Tokyo:

```
var now = new Date();

var jpn = "Tokyo Time :\n"+now.toString()+"\n\n";

var gmt = "UTC Time :\n" + now.toGMTString();

alert(jpn + gmt);
```

Using The System Clock

When a JavaScript is needed to create an action repeatedly in a web browser window the system clock can be used with the JavaScript "setTimeout()" method of the window object.

This method may run a function after a given delay.

Two arguments are required stating the name of the function to call and the required delay time in milliseconds.

This method is often used at the end of a function to call the same function recursively, following a set delay.

There is a slide-show script on page 166 using this method.

Many uses can be found for this method in creating dynamic effects such as with slide show scripts where the function displays successive images at given intervals.

The example here uses the window.setTimeout() method to display an alert dialog box at 10 second intervals:

```
var num = 0;

function annoy(){

num++;

alert( "This is 10-Second Message No: " +num );

window.setTimeout( "annoy()" , 10000);

}

annoy();
```

Call the timer function after it has been declared to start the timer.

Cancelling The Timer

The unfortunate viewer of the site containing the JavaScript on the previous page would doubtless feel aggrieved at the constant alert box messages. It may be better to show the message only a couple of times then stop the function.

The setTimeout() method can be cancelled easily using the "clearTimeout()" method of the window object.

In order to clear the timer correctly it is necessary to assign the original setTimeout() call to a variable so that the variable can be passed to the clearTimeout() call arguments.

The following example displays a message twice then displays a final message when the timer is cleared:

The variable name "tim" is often used to name the timer variable.

```
var num = 0, tim;

function advise(){
num++;
if( num == 3 ){
alert( "OK - I told you twice" );
window.clearTimeout( tim );
} else {
alert( "This is 10-Second Message No : " + num );
tim = window.setTimeout( "advise()" , 10000); }
}

advise();
```

JavaScript Clock

Utilising the date object along with a timer can create a time display that updates every second to produce a clock.

The example below displays the local time dynamically in a html form text input:

The clock needs to be started from an onload call in the html <body> tag.

```
<HTML>
<BODY ONLOAD = "tick()" >
<SCRIPT TYPE = "text/javascript" >
<!--

function tick(){
var now = new Date();
var hh = now.getHours();    if( hh <= 9 ) hh = "0" + hh;
var mn = now.getMinutes(); if( mn <= 9 ) mn = "0" + mn;
var ss = now.getSeconds(); if( ss <= 9 ) ss = "0" + ss;
var tt = hh + ": " +mn+ ": " + ss;
document.f.clock.value = tt;
window.setTimeout( "tick()", 1000 );
}

//-->
</SCRIPT>
<FORM NAME = "f" >
<INPUT NAME= "clock" TYPE = "text" SIZE = "10">
</FORM>
</BODY>
</HTML>
```

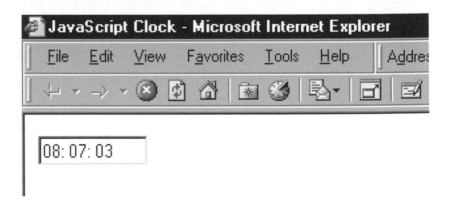

Doing Mathematics

This chapter is devoted to the JavaScript Math object and describes the constant values and methods that are available to perform mathematical calculations. The subject of random number generation is covered and is illustrated with a practical example using random values.

Covers

Chapter Six

Math Constants

The intrinsic JavaScript Math object contains a number of standard mathematical constant values for easy reference.

Uppercase is always used to refer to the constant values which are all listed in the following table:

Observe correct capitalization when using any of the Math constants.

Math.E	The constant e base of the natural logarithm with a value of approximately 2.71828
Math.LN2	The natural logarithm of 2 approximately 0.69314718055994528623
Math.LN10	The natural logarithm of 10 approximately 2.30258509299404459011
Math.LOG2E	The base-2 logarithm of e approximately 1.442695040888963387
Math.LOG10E	The base-10 logarithm of e approximately 0.43429448190325181677
Math.PI	The constant pi approximately 3.14159265358979
Math.SQRT1_2	The reciprocal of the square root of 2 approximately 0.7071067811865476
Math.SQRT2	The square root of 2 with a value of approximately 1.414213562373095

The Math constants can be used anywhere within a script.

Most of the Math constants are used only in JavaScript applications that have a particular mathematical purpose but the full list is given above for completeness.

Using Pi

The Math.PI constant creates interesting possibilities with dynamic effects. The following example script dynamically rotates four layers named "lyr0", "lyr1", "lyr2" and "lyr3":

 The Math.cos() and Math.sin() methods used in this example are just some of the Math object methods detailed on the next page.

```
var pos = new Array();      // array for position data
var xos = 30, yos = 30;     // xy coordinate offsets
var rad = 40;               // radius of circle

function init(){
for(var i = 0; i < 4; i++ ){
pos[i] = ( i == 0 ) ? 0 : parseFloat( pos[i-1] +
(( 2 * Math.PI ) / 4 )); }  spin();
}

function spin(){
for(var i = 0; i < 4 ; i++){
pos[i] += Math.PI / 45;           // increment degrees
var x = xos + (rad * Math.cos( pos[i] ));
var y = yos +( rad * Math.sin( pos[i] ));
if(document.layers)document.layers["lyr"+i].moveTo(x,y);
if(document.all)
eval( "lyr"+i+".style.top=x; lyr"+i+".style.left=y" );
}
setTimeout("spin()",100);
}
```

 The "moveTo" layer method seen here is Netscape-only so the code has a seperate statement to run the spin in Internet Explorer.

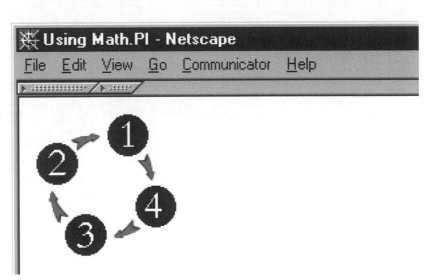

Math Methods

The Math JavaScript object has many methods and all are listed in the table below:

Math.abs()	return an absolute value
Math.acos()	return an arc cosine
Math.asin()	return an arc sine
Math.atan()	return an arc tangent
Math.atan2()	return angle from an X-axis to a point
Math.ceil()	round a number up
Math.cos()	return a cosine value
Math.exp()	return an exponent of constant e
Math.floor()	round a number down
Math.log()	return a natural logarithm
Math.max()	return the larger of two numbers
Math.min()	return the smaller of two numbers
Math.pow()	return the power value
Math.random()	return a random number
Math.round()	round to the nearest integer
Math.sin()	return a sine value
Math.sqrt()	return the sqaure root
Math.tan()	return a tangent value

Math.random() has many uses in web pages to provide varied page content.

The Math methods most commonly used from the above list are examined in more detail on the following pages.

Rounding Floats

The Math.round() method in JavaScript is useful both to round floating-point numbers to the nearest integer and commute long floating-point numbers to shorter rounded versions. Commonly this will be to reduce a long floating-point number to two decimal places.

If the floating point value given as the method argument is exactly halfway between two integers the method will round up to the nearest integer.

The example given below illustrates the way that the Math.round() method handles rounding of positive and negative halfway values and shows how it may be used to commute a long floating-point number to just two places:

Rounding -7.5 does not result -8.0 because that would be a higher negative number, and so that would be rounding down.

```javascript
var a = 7.5;
a = Math.round(a);
a = "Rounded Positive : "+a+ "\n";

var b = -7.5;
b = Math.round(b);
b = "Rounded Negative : "+b+ "\n";

var c = 3.764638467915;
c = c * 100;                // take it up two places
c = Math.round(c);          // do the round
c /= 100;                   // take it back down 2 places
c = "Commuted Long Float : "+c;
alert( a+b+c );
```

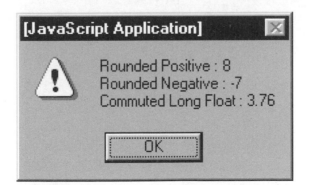

Forcing Floats

As an alternative to using the Math.round() method detailed on the previous page the script may require that the float be selectively forced to the nearest integer above or below.

JavaScript provides the Math.ceil() method to force rounding up to the nearest integer and the Math.floor() method rounds to the nearest integer down.

The example below illustrates both methods in action with both positive and negative values:

Rounding up of negative values returns a next nearest integer towards zero.

```
var a = 7.5;

var a1 = "a1 : " + Math.ceil(a);

var a2 = "a2 : " + Math.floor(a);

var b = -7.5;

var b1 = "b1 : " + Math.ceil(b);

var b2 = "b2 : " + Math.floor(b);

var rup = "ROUNDING UP\n" +a1+ "\n" +b1+ "\n\n";

var rdn = "ROUNDING DOWN\n" +a2+ "\n" +b2;

alert( rup+rdn );
```

Comparing Numbers

The Math object has two methods allowing comparison of two numbers with a return of the higher or lower value.

Math.max() accepts the two values for comparison as arguments and will return the higher of the two values.

The Math.min() method works in precisely the same way but returns the lower of the two given values.

In the example below the Math.pow() method is used to create square and cube values that are then compared with Math.max() and Math.min().

The Math.pow() method requires two arguments to specify the number then the power by which to raise that number:

```
var sq = Math.pow( 5, 2 );

var cb = Math.pow( 3, 3 )

var hi = "Round up : " + Math.max( sq, cb );

var lo = "Round Down : " + Math.min( sq, cb );

var ng = "Round Negative Up : " + Math.max( -5, -4.75 );

alert( "MAXMIN\n\n" + hi + "\n" + lo + "\n" + ng);
```

The higher of two negative numbers is the one closest to zero.

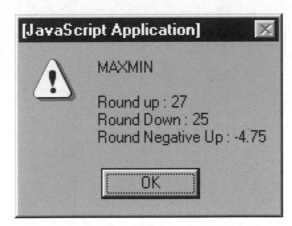

Random Generator

Random numbers can be generated using the Math.random() method to return a floating-point value between 0.0 and 1.0.

This method can be used to create a series of random number selections, like a lottery draw, and is popular for producing random effects within web pages.

Multiplying the random number will specify a wider range so, for example, a multiplier of 10 will create a random number now between 0.0 and 10.0.

To make the randomly generated number more useful it is generally best to round up the returned float so that the range will become two integer values.

The Math.ceil() method will be used to round the random number up to an integer between 1 and 10 inclusive.

The code below illustrates this example:

The individual steps are shown with the rand variables but the normal syntax is used with the variable named another.

```
var rand1 = Math.random();
var rand2 = rand1 * 10;
var rand3 = Math.ceil( rand3 );

var another = Math.ceil( Math.random() * 10 );
```

[JavaScript Application]

RANDOMS

Random Float (rand1) : 0.30151709839283797
Specify Range (rand2) : 3.0151709839283797
Random Integer (rand3) : 3

Another Random : 7

OK

Lottery Picker

This example uses Math.random() to generate a series of six random numbers within the range of 1 to 49 which can be used as selections in the national UK lottery:

```javascript
var n = new Array(6);

for(var i=0; i<6; i++){ n[i] = "";}

while(n[5] == ""){
var j = Math.ceil(Math.random()*49);

if(n[0]=="")n[0]= j;
else
if(n[1]==""&&j!=n[0])n[1]=j;
else
if(n[2]==""&&j!=n[0]&&j!=n[1])n[2]=j;
else
if(n[3]==""&&j!=n[0]&&j!=n[1]&&j!=n[2])n[3]=j;
else
if(n[4]==""&&j!=n[0]&&j!=n[1]&&j!=n[2]&&j!=n[3])n[4]=j;
else
if(n[5]==""&&j!=n[0]&&j!=n[1]&&j!=n[2]&&j!=n[3]&&j!=n[4])
n[5] = j;
}

var str = "";
for (i=0; i<6; i++){ str += n[i] + "  "; }

alert( "LUCKY NUMBERS\n\n" + str);
```

The random numbers are placed into the "n" array only if they have not been previously selected.

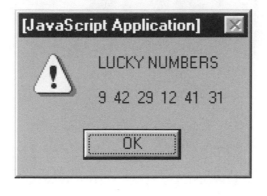

Random Images

The Math.random() method is used in the following example that is placed in the body section of an html page. The JavaScript displays an image, for an html img tag with a name attribute value of "pic", that is determined by the code each time the page is loaded and the script is executed.

Document Properties and Methods are fully explained in Chapter 10.

```
<SCRIPT TYPE = "text/javascript">
<!--

var pix = new Array( "pic0.gif", "pic1.gif", "pic2.gif",
"pic3.gif", "pic4.gif", "pic5.gif", "pic6.gif" );

var rand = Math.floor(Math.random() * 7);

document.images.pic.src = pix[ rand ];

document.write(rand + " : " + pix[ rand ]);

//-->
</SCRIPT>
```

Use this script to randomly display banners on a web page.

JavaScript selected the image below :

3 : pic3.gif

The image may differ when the page next loads.

Working With Strings

This chapter explains string characteristics and demonstrates by example how text strings may be manipulated with JavaScript code.

Covers

Chapter Seven

String Length

A string in JavaScript is simply zero or more characters enclosed within quotes, so these are all strings:

```
var str1 = "My First String";

var str2 = "";

var str3 = "2";

var str4 = "null";
```

The empty quotes in "str2" define the variable as being a string data type regardless of the empty string value. The numeric value assigned to "str3" is automatically converted to a string when enclosed in quotes and the JavaScript "null" keyword is just a string literal when enclosed by quotes.

Essentially a string is a collection of characters, each character containing its own data, just like elements in a defined array.

It is logical to regard a string as an array of characters and apply array characteristics when using strings.

The example below parallels the array.length property with the string.length property:

```
var a = "JavaScript Strings";

alert( a.length );
```

Spaces are counted as a character too.

Characters In Strings

Strings are just arrays where each element is a character and can be referenced in the same way as regular array elements.

So just like arrays the first character is element 0(zero).

The characters can be found using the string.charAt() method which takes the element index number as its sole argument.

The example below reads the characters in a string and makes changes according to the character found:

This method can be used for simple string validation of an email address by seeking an "@" character.

```
var str = "linger in", newstr = "";

var a = "First letter : " + str.charAt( 0 );

var z = "Final letter : " + str.charAt( str.length -1 );

for( var i = 0; i < str.length; i++ ){

if( str.charAt( i ) != "i" ) newstr += str.charAt( i );

else newstr += "o";

}

var result = "STRINGS\n\n";

result += "New string : " + newstr + "\n";

alert( result + a + "\n" + z );
```

Join Strings

The "+" operator is used to concatenate strings and is widely used in the example code given throughout this book.

A new string is created that consists of the first string followed immediately by the second string.

The example below concatenates a number of variable values into a single string, irrespective of the original data type, because JavaScript performs automatic data type conversion:

Remember to escape quotes if included inside a string.

```
var num = 99;

var flt = 98.6;

var bool = true;

var str1 = "Although ";

var str2 = " F is cited as \"body temperature\" ";

var str3 = "\nthe ";

var str4 = " range is from about 97 to ";

var str5 = " F.";

alert( str1 +flt +str2 +str3 +bool +str4 +num +str5 );
```

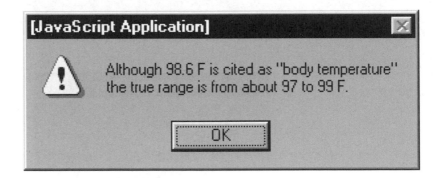

Search A String

JavaScript can search a string to find a character or substring passed as the argument to the string.indexOf() method.

If a match is made the method returns the starting position of the first occurrence of the matched character or substring within the searched string.

In the event that no match is found the string.indexOf() method returns a value of -1.

The following example uses the string.indexOf() method to seek a dot and @ character within an email address string to perform a simple format validation:

An optional second integer argument may specify the position from which to start the search.

```javascript
var str= "mailme@domain.com";

var att = str.indexOf("@");

var dot = str.indexOf(".");

var hsh = str.indexOf("#");

var fmt = ((att != -1)&&(dot != -1))? "valid":"invalid";

var res = "Format is " +fmt;
res += "\n@ at " +att;
res += "\nDot at " +dot;
res += "\n\nHash is " +hsh;

alert(res);
```

Separate Words

The contents of a string may be separated using the JavaScript string.split() method.

A single argument should specify a common character for a delimiter at which points the string will be separated.

Most commonly this can be a single space character so that a phrase with normal spacing will be separated into an array of single words.

Each of the words can then be referenced using the index number of the split string array, like any other array.

The example below illustrates this use of the string.split() method together with another instance where items in a database may use a pipe character as the delimiter:

Data is often stored as a comma-delimited string.

```
var str = "JavaScript in easy steps";

var ss = str.split( " " );

var bk = "JavaScript in easy steps|Mike McGrath|£9.99";

var bks  = bk.split("|");

var res = "Topic : " +  ss[0];
res += "\nTitle : " + bks[0];
res += "\nAuthor : " + bks[1];
res += "\nPrice : " + bks[2];

alert(res);
```

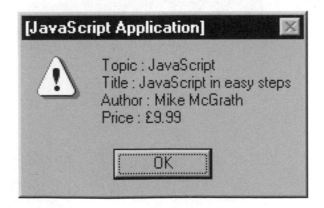

Substrings

A substring may be extracted from an existing string using the string.substring() method which must have two arguments to specify the start and end positions of the required substring within the main string.

The character at the start argument position will be the first character in the returned substring. The last character in the substring will be the character preceding the given end argument position.

An alternative way to extract a substring from a string is available with the string.substr() method which also requires two arguments. While the first argument again specifies the start position of the substring the second will specify the length of the substring to be returned.

The example below demonstrates both substring methods:

The substr() method will invariably be easiest to use.

```
var str = "JavaScript in easy steps";

var sub1 = str.substring(14,19) +  str.substring(0,11)

var sub2 = str.substr(14,5) + str.substr(0,10);

var res = "Substring method : " +sub1;

res += "\nSubstr method : " +sub2;

alert(res);
```

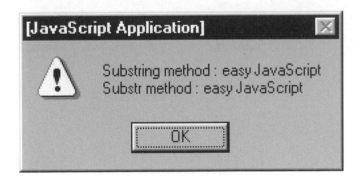

Convert To String

It is possible to manually call the JavaScript function that is used to convert other data types to strings by calling the object.toString() method.

This is an essential JavaScript function and will always try to return a string representation of the object that is being queried, even if it is not itself a string.

In this example there is firstly a straightforward addition of two integers, followed by a concatenation of a string with an integer where the integer is converted to a string value.

Finally the object.toString() method is demonstrated with a different data type to illustrate that the generated output will reveal the object type.

The toString() method can be used anywhere in JavaScript to reveal some information about an object.

```
var num = 9;

var nostr = num + 9;

var adstr= num.toString() + 9;

var img = new Image();

var res = "No strings : " + nostr;

res += "\nAdded strings : " + adstr;

res += "\nImage : " + img.toString();

alert(res);
```

Change Case

The string character case may be changed using the string.toUpperCase() or string.toLowerCase() methods to force all the characters to become a common case.

Be sure to have the correct capitalization when using these methods.

These methods are most useful when comparing user input to ensure that the character format agrees with the comparison format.

In the following example the string.toLowerCase() method converts a user entry in a form text field for comparison with a string variable value that is in lower case:

```
var entry = document.forms[0].textfield.value;

if(entry.toLowerCase() == "castle") alert("Accepted");

else alert("Refused");
```

See page 125 for fuller details on referencing form elements.

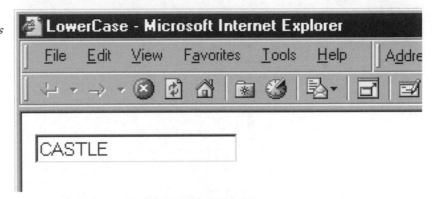

Numbers From Strings

A number can be extracted from the beginning of a string with the parseInt() and parseFloat() methods.

The parseInt() method parses the string and returns the first integer value that is located while the parseFloat() method works in the same way but returns a floating point number.

If the parser finds any non-numeric character before returning a number then it will return the special "NaN" value that is used to denote "Not- a-Number".

This example demonstrates both parseFloat() and parseInt() methods and illustrates the JavaScript isNaN() function testing for a "NaN" value:

The "NaN" value cannot be tested for with the == equality operator.

```
var str = "66.6% PASS RATE";

var res = "Integer : " + parseInt(str);

res += "\nFloat : " + parseFloat(str);

var badstr = "PASS RATE 66.6%";

res += "\nNon-numeric : " + parseInt(badstr);

res += "\nFound : ";

res += isNaN( parseInt(badstr) )? "Character": "Number";

alert(res);
```

Variables In Strings

The JavaScript eval() function accepts as an argument a string containing JavaScript code which it evaluates and returns the resulting value.

If the code string contains statements they will be executed by the eval() function and the final value will be returned.

While this function is a powerful feature of the JavaScript language it is most often used to introduce variable values into a string.

In the example below the script assigns a string value to be displayed in a form text box that has been named "textfield" in the html code.

The text box name and the display string are stored in variables that are evaluated by the eval() function.

Remember to escape the quotes inside a string to avoid error messages.

```javascript
var inputname = "textfield";

var inputtext = " \"JavaScript Text\" ";

eval("document.forms[0]."+inputname+".value="+inputtext);
```

Now the text string is displayed in the text field because the code string evaluates to:

```javascript
document.forms[0].textfield.value = "JavaScript Text";
```

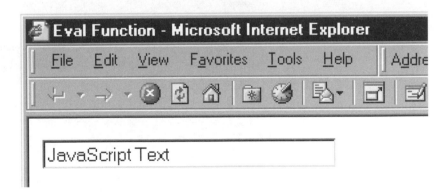

Encoding Strings

All characters have a Unicode numerical representation that can be returned for each individual character in a string with the string.charCodeAt() method. This method requires the index of the character within the string as it's argument.

Conversely characters can be extracted from Unicode using the JavaScript String.fromCharCode() function that takes the unicode numeric values as its argument.

The example below first loops through a string and makes a comma delimited string of it's Unicode character values.

An array of these Unicode numeric values is then created for the second loop to return the character for each number:

Notice that the fromCharCode() function is a property of the String() constructor and is not a string object method.

```
var str = "Code Fun";
var enc = "";
var unc = "";

for( var i = 0; i < str.length; i++ ) {
enc += str.charCodeAt( i ) + ",";
}

var ss = enc.split( "," );

for( i = 0; i < ss.length; i++ ) {
unc += String.fromCharCode( ss[i] );
}

alert( "Encoded : " +enc+ "\nUnencoded : " +unc );
```

Addressing Page Objects

Following on from the JavaScript language foundation this chapter starts to explore how scripts may communicate with various aspects of a web page using the browser Document Object Model (DOM). Many common uses of the top-level "navigator" object are demonstrated.

Covers

Chapter Eight

Object Constructor

The JavaScript syntax to address object properties and methods uses the object name followed by a period then the property name.

For example, array.length addresses the length property of the array object.

Previous example code in this book has used intrinsic JavaScript objects with pre-defined properties and methods.

New custom objects can easily be created though using the JavaScript "new" keyword with the Object() constructor.

Properties may then be allocated to the new custom object by declaring a property name and assigning a value to it.

The example below creates a new object called car and then gives it three properties with assigned values:

To declare a property use both the object name and given property name.

```
var car = new Object();

car.maker = "Porsche";

car.model = "Boxster";

car.color = "Red";

alert( car.color + " " + car.maker + " " + car.model );
```

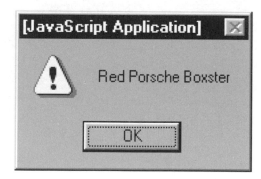

Property Inheritance

Further flexibility can be added to the example on the facing page by assigning the newly created custom object to a property of another custom object.

In this case the properties and values of the assigned object are inherited by the property of the second custom object.

The inherited properties are addressed by adding a period and the inherited property name after the property address to which they have been assigned.

It is helpful to understand this relationship when dealing with objects and properties in web pages.

The following example demonstrates how a new object is assigned to a property of a second custom object and how the inherited properties may then be addressed:

 An object must have first been created in the script before it can be assigned to another object's property.

```javascript
var mondeo = new Object();
mondeo.badge = "Mondeo";
mondeo.body = "Saloon";
mondeo.doors = 4;
mondeo.color = "Red";
mondeo.engine = "1.8 litre";

var car = new Object();
car.maker = "Ford";
car.model = mondeo;

alert(car.maker+" "+car.model.badge+" "+car.model.body);
```

[JavaScript Application]

⚠ Ford Mondeo Saloon

OK

DOM Hierarchy

The browser Document Object Model (DOM) is a collection of objects in a web browser that can be addressed by JavaScript in order to influence the performance of a html document.

These objects follow a strict hierarchy where the "window" object is the very top level and a fuller picture of the DOM hierarchy is depicted on page 178 of this book.

A "self" syntax may be used to address the window, such as self.bgColor.

Because "window" is the top level object it can be omitted in the address syntax so that the window.document.bgColor property, which stores the value of the window's current background colour, can be addressed as document.bgColor.

Several of the DOM objects have properties to contain an array of the elements in that web page. For example, with document.images[] the images[] array is a property of the "document" object that will store the url of each image contained on that web page.

The url of the first image in the html code is stored in the array at document.images[0] then the url of successive images are stored at incrementing array element indexes.

All of the code examples in this book have been tested with Netscape and Internet Explorer DOMs.

Unfortunately the DOM is not standard across browsers so the Netscape DOM is different to the more comprehensive DOM used by Microsoft Internet Explorer.

This example assigns a value to the document.bgColor:

```
document.bgColor = "black";
```

Revealing Page Objects

The script example below reveals the default window objects in both Internet Explorer 5.5 and Netscape 4.7.

This script can show further DOM objects - try replacing 'window' with 'document' to see more.

```
for( propertyName in window )

document.write( propertyName + ", " );
```

IE5.5 window objects - Microsoft Internet Explorer

File   Edit   View   Favorites   Tools   Help

onbeforeunload, onafterprint, top, location,
parent, offscreenBuffering, frameElement, onerror,
screen, event, clipboardData, onresize,
defaultStatus, onblur, window, onload,
onscroll, screenTop, onfocus, Option,
length, onbeforeprint, frames, self,
clientInformation, external, screenLeft, opener,
onunload, document, closed, history,
Image, navigator, status, onhelp,
name,

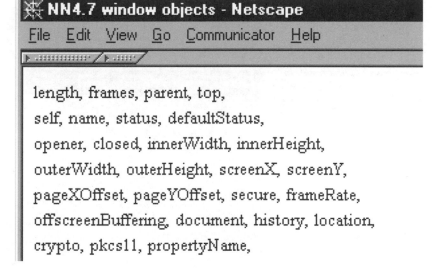

NN4.7 window objects - Netscape

File   Edit   View   Go   Communicator   Help

length, frames, parent, top,
self, name, status, defaultStatus,
opener, closed, innerWidth, innerHeight,
outerWidth, outerHeight, screenX, screenY,
pageXOffset, pageYOffset, secure, frameRate,
offscreenBuffering, document, history, location,
crypto, pkcs11, propertyName,

Browser ID

The navigator object has properties that provide information about the browser that is being used to view a document.

The browser name is revealed by the navigator.appName property whereas the particular version is available from the navigator.appVersion property.

In addition to the release number the navigator.appVersion property may contain further optional details.

The Microsoft output in the following example provides additional information of the user platform. Netscape also adds the user language and encryption detail:

```javascript
var browser = navigator.appName;

var version = navigator.appVersion;

alert( browser + "\n" + version );
```

Notice that the release version of this browser is Internet Explorer 5.5.

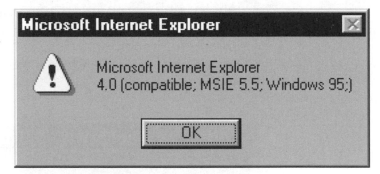

The final data in the return is a capital 'i' that denotes an International version encryption level.

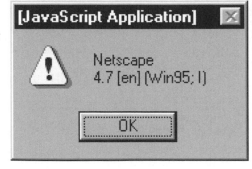

Cross-Browser Compliancy

In order for web pages to display as desired it is often necessary to get browser id so that a browser-specific page can be loaded or browser-specific code can be applied.

Release 4.0 of both major browsers added new properties to the document object to enable dynamic effects in dhtml. Netscape introduced the document.layers property while Microsoft created the document.all property.

It is often convenient to test for these to identify the browser and ensure that it is dhtml-capable.

The following example performs this check and opens a browser-specific page accordingly for modern Netscape browsers, modern Microsoft browsers, old Netscape browsers or a default page for any other browsers:

The location property of the window object holds current page location so changing its value will also load a new location.

```
if(document.all) window.location = "ie-dhtml.html";

if(document.layers) window.location = "nn-dhtml.html";

else {
var oldnn = ( navigator.appName == "Netscape"
&& parseInt( navigator.appVersion ) < 4 );
location = ( oldnn ) ? "nn-old.html" : "default.html";
}
```

This shows the page loaded by the script after it has run in Netscape 3.04.

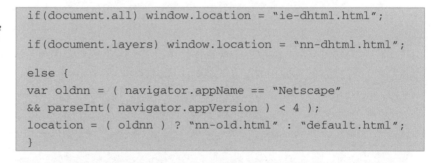

This is the page for older Netscape browsers...
it will run JavaScript
but it does not support Dynamic HTML

Platform Check

The performance of a web page may be affected by the operating system on which the browser is running due to some lack of support for the page content.

ActiveX controls are one way to create interface features on web documents.

For example, Windows version 3.1 does not support ActiveX so any web pages containing an ActiveX control will not perform as intended on that platform.

Also some dhtml effects that run fine in Internet Explorer on a PC platform may not appear correctly in the equivalent Internet Explorer version on a Mac system.

Platform-specific scripting can be achieved, in a similar manner to that used for browser-specific scripting, with the navigator.platform property.

This property contains a short string representing the user's operating system and can be read to branch the script to accommodate any platform limitations.

The example below simply writes a line of text according to the platform located:

```
if(navigator.platform == "Win16" )var os= "Windows 3.1";

if(navigator.platform == "Mac" ) os = "MacOS";

if(navigator.platform == "Win32") os = "Windows 95";

document.write ( "Operating system is " + os);
```

Shockwave Test

JavaScript may check to see if the user can view a Macromedia Flash movie and load an alternative page if the Shockwave plugin is unavailable.

Any version of Internet Explorer running on a platform other than Mac or Windows 3.1 will support Flash so the script can identify the browser then exclude these platforms.

The navigator.plugins property can be used in Netscape browsers to seek the Shockwave Flash plugin directly but this property is not fully supported in Internet Explorer.

The example below performs these tests then loads an appropriate page depending on the result:

```
if( (navigator.appName == "Microsoft Internet Explorer"
&& navigator.appVersion.indexOf( "Mac" ) == -1
&& navigator.appVersion.indexOf( "3.1" ) == -1)
||
(navigator.plugins
&& navigator.plugins["Shockwave Flash"])
|| navigator.plugins["Shockwave Flash 2.0"] )
window.location = "playflash.html";
else
window.location = "noflash.html";
```

For more Flash and Shockwave info visit the Macromedia website at www.macromedia.com.

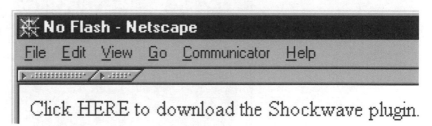

Java Detection

A browser can be assessed for Java enablement using the navigator.javaEnabled() method to return a boolean value of true or false depending on the result.

This can be used to determine if a page containing a Java applet should be loaded or if an alternative non-Java page should be loaded instead.

The example below demonstrates Java detection:

```
if ( navigator.javaEnabled() )
window.location = "javapage.html";
else
window.location = "nonjavapage.html";
```

Notice that as javaEnabled() is a method of the navigator object, not merely a property, it must have following brackets.

Window Properties

This chapter demonstrates properties and methods of the window object. Creating popup windows is illustrated and the use of framed pages is also discussed with examples of how to address objects in other frames.

Covers

Chapter Nine

Confirm

The alert() function that is used extensively in the code examples given throughout this book is actually a method of the top-level window object so may be correctly addressed as window.alert().

The window.confirm() method is the first of two other window methods that produce dialog boxes when called.

It is used to get user confirmation from a dialog box containing an OK button that returns true to the script and a Cancel button that returns false to the script.

A single argument should be passed to the method as a text string containing the question for the user to confirm.

This example demonstrates the window.confirm() method performing conditional branching to determine which message string to write dependant upon which button the user pushes in the confirm dialog box:

In this example (ask) is simply shorthand for (ask == true).

```
var ask = confirm( "Do you wish to proceed ?" );

var msg;

if( ask ) msg = "OK button was pushed";

else msg = "Cancel button was pushed";

document.write( msg );
```

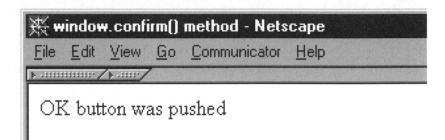

Prompt

The window.prompt() method is used to get keyboard input from the user through a dialog box containing a textfield together with OK and Cancel buttons.

Two string arguments are required by the window.prompt() method to specify a message to display and a default textfield value. The second argument should be an empty string if no default textfield value is needed by the script.

The dialog box returns the value of the textfield when the users push the OK button as seen in this example that takes user input to personalise the page content:

This script assigns the "visitor" value if no user name is entered.

```
var user = prompt( "Please enter your name...", "" );

if(user == null || user == "" ) user = "visitor";

document.write( "Hi " +user+ ", welcome to this page");
```

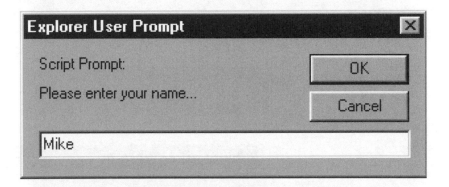

Location

The window.location object contains the full url of the document that is currently loaded in the browser.

It stores the full url address in the window.location.href property and assigning a new value to this or to the window.location object itself will load the given url into the browser.

A typical url address may comprise of these parts:

```
protocol: // host / pathname ? # hash
```

Each part of the url address stored in the window.location object may be addressed individually using the appropriate location property as seen in the example given below:

Assigning a new value to location.hash will move the browser to the given location in the page.

```
var locn = "Href : " + location.href;

var prot = "Protocol : " + location.protocol;

var host = "Host : " + location.host;

var path = "Path : " + location.pathname;

var hash = "Hash : " + location.hash;

alert(locn+"\n"+prot+"\n"+host+"\n"+path+"\n"+hash);
```

History

The window.history object contains an array of the url addresses previously visited during a browser session.

For security reasons they are not directly readable but they are used to navigate back to previous pages.

The back() and forward() methods of the window.history object emulate the browser's Back and Forward buttons.

More flexible navigation is often provided by the window.history.go() method that takes a single argument to specify the location by relative position.

For example, an argument value of -1 will revisit the previous page and a value of -2 reopens the page before it.

In a similar manner window.history.go(1) goes forward to the next page in the history array of visited urls.

Calling window.history.go(0) causes the browser to reload the current document.

The example below returns the user to a previous page if the user has omitted to complete a required textfield:

This example assumes that the required input value has been stored in a data-persistent state for retrieval by the script code - see cookies on page 114.

```
if( required_input == "" ) history.go( -1 );
```

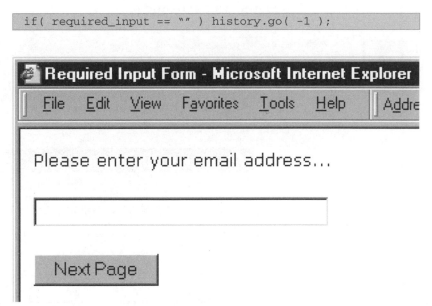

Onload

The window.onload object may be used to specify the name of a function to be called immediately after a document has completely loaded in a browser.

Typically this initializing function is named "init()" and is often used to set a number of values within the script.

The slideshow script on page 166 does not start to run until called by onload when all the images have downloaded.

It is especially useful when the page contains a large number of graphics that may take a while to download. If these images are used by the script it is essential that they finish downloading before the script starts to run.

The html onload attribute, that may optionally be included in the html body tag, also specifies the onload function so care is needed to avoid overwriting one with the other.

This is again the case with the window.onunload object and the html onunload attribute which can both specify a function to call when the user navigates to a new location.

Frequently window.onunload calls a function that creates a popup window when the user leaves a website.

This example displays a simple alert dialog message when the user exits the page:

The assigned value is the name of the function so the argument brackets are not required

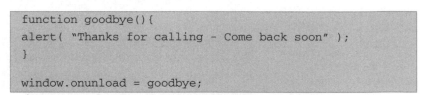

```
function goodbye(){
alert( "Thanks for calling - Come back soon" );
}

window.onunload = goodbye;
```

Status

The window.status object can be used to display a message in the status bar of the browser window until another feature in the displayed document sets a new status bar message or the status bar is returned to its default state.

A default message to display can be specified with the window.defaultStatus object.

See more about onmouseover & other events in Chapter 12.

To display a message when the user places the cursor over a hyperlink the html onmouseover attribute should specify the message to display. It must also return true to prevent the link url appearing in the status bar as it would do normally.

This example, using JavaScript within html tags, specifies a default message and adds an onmouseover attribute to the link that will display another message while the cursor remains over the link:

```
<BODY ONLOAD = "window.defaultStatus = 'Status Demo'" >

<A HREF = "nextpage.htm"
ONMOUSEOVER = "window.status='Click Here';return true" >
Hypertext Link</A>
```

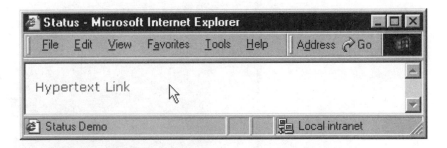

Pop-Up Window

One of the most useful browser features provided by JavaScript is the ability to open a second browser window displaying another url.

This is possible using the window.open() method which takes three arguments to specify the url to load in the pop-up window, a name for the pop-up and its desired features.

These pop-up windows are invariably smaller than the original window and have many uses including the display of large images from a display of thumbnail-sized images.

The example below opens a secondary pop-up window following complete loading of the first window:

The second argument must be an empty string if no name is being given to the pop-up window.

```
function popup(){

window.open( "popup.html", "",
"top=40,left=40,width=200,height=100");

}

window.onload = popup;
```

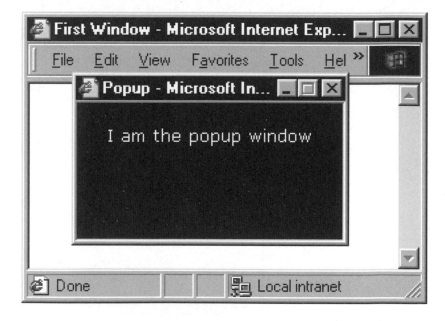

Pop-Up Features

The third argument to the window.open() method may specify many features to be included in the new window from the list in the following table:

See the code example on the next page that adds some of these features.

Feature	Description
directories	Adds the links bar
height	Sets the height in pixels of the document area
left	The X co-ordinate of the window on the screen
location	Adds the address bar
menubar	Adds the standard menu bar
resizable	Permits the window to be resized
scrollbars	Enables scrollbars when needed
status	Adds the status bar
toolbar	Adds the button bar with back & forward buttons
top	The Y co-ordinate of the window on the screen
width	Sets the width in pixels of the document area

The list of features should have comma separators but not any spaces.

The dimension features of top, left, width and height need to state a pixel value like the example on the facing page.

All the other features can have a value of "yes" or "no" but if the feature appears in the argument a "yes" value is assumed so the value need not be specified.

For example, to add a status bar to the code on the facing page just requires the addition of status to the features list:

```
function popup(){
window.open( "popup.html", "",
"top=40,left=40,width=200,height=100,status");
}
```

Close Pop-Up

A window can close itself simply by calling the window.close() method but closing a pop-up window requires a little more effort.

The initial call to the window.open() method should be assigned to a variable to create a window object.

Notice that the spelling of the resizable feature is not "resizeable".

This new window object inherits the window.close() method which can be used to close the pop-up window.

The example verifies the existence of the pop-up window before closing it when the user exits the main window:

```
var popwindow;

function popup(){
popwindow = window.open( "popup.html", "",
"top=40,left=40,width=200,height=100,directories,
location,menubar,resizable,scrollbars,toolbar");
}

function close_popup(){
if( popwindow != null )popwindow.close();
}

window.onload = popup;
window.onunload = close_popup;
```

Small windows with too many features appear too cluttered.

Get Size

It is sometimes useful to have JavaScript get the user's screen resolution from the width and height properties of the window.screen object.

Because a window may not be maximized to the full screen size it is also helpful to determine the actual inner width of the window.

The availHeight and availWidth properties of window.screen contain screen size excluding task bars.

The Netscape and Internet Explorer document object models have different ways of storing inner window dimensions so browser-specific scripting is needed.

In the example below JavaScript finds the resolution and window inner size for both browsers of version 4 or later:

```
if(document.all){        // Internet Explorer
var win_w = window.document.body.clientWidth;
var win_h = window.document.body.clientHeight;
}
if(document.layers){    // Netscape
win_w = window.innerWidth;
win_h = window.innerHeight;
}

if(document.all || document.layers){
var scr_w = window.screen.width;
var scr_h = window.screen.height;
var res = "Resolution :" + scr_w + " x " + scr_h;
var iwin = "Inner window : " + win_w + " x " +win_h;
alert( res + "\n" + iwin );
}
```

Call the window.print() method to print out the document in the browser window.

Frames Array

The window.frames object contains an array of all the frames in a window which have been defined in the html frameset tags.

Javascript can address these from within any frame using the parent.window.frames[] syntax.

Individual frames can be addressed using their index number in the array or the value assigned to the name attribute in the html frame tag. So a frame named "main" can be addressed from within another frame by parent.window.frames.main.

The example code below runs from a frame to read the names of all the frames in the window:

Always naming html elements to be used by JavaScript will produce code that is more easily readable.

```
var framenums = "No. frames : "
+parent.window.frames.length;

var framenames= "\nFrame 1 : "
+parent.window.frames[0].name;

framenames+= "\nFrame 2 : "
+parent.window.frames[1].name;

framenames+= "\nFrame 3 : "
+parent.window.frames[2].name;

alert(framenums + framenames);
```

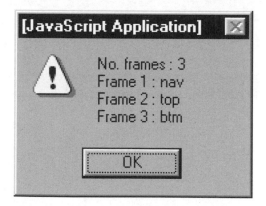

Frame Objects

The example on the facing page allows access to different frames within a framed window and because the browser DOM is hierarchical that means that the objects and properties within any frame are also accessible.

The script can assign values to these object properties and use their methods just as with an unframed window.

Typically a navigation frame on the left side of the window will have buttons which, when pushed, will assign new url locations to a main frame on the right side of the screen.

This example extends the one on the facing page with code in the "nav" frame both writing text to the "hdr" frame and adding a function to change the location of the "btm" frame:

Notice that the script writes a html tag along with the text.

```
function next(){
parent.frames.btm.window.location = "nextpage.htm";
}

function write_header(){
var msg = "Frame 2 <br>Written by Frame 1";
parent.frames.hdr.window.document.write( msg );
}

window.onload = write_header;
```

Error Handling

A custom error-handling function may be assigned to the window.onerror object to deal with runtime errors.

When the browser meets an error it looks for an error handler in the script but, if none is found, it will handle the error itself by opening the browser error dialog box.

Once the error has been notified a true value is returned to the browser to indicate that the error has been dealt with.

To avoid all error dialogs a custom error-handling function need only return true when an error is encountered.

Usefully the browser will pass three arguments to the error handler containing information on the nature of the error, the url of the file that contains the error and the actual line number in that file where the error exists.

In the example below each piece of error information passed to the error-handling function by the browser is displayed for the benefit of the user:

The error handler must be declared at the top of the script block to catch all possible errors.

```
window.onerror = errorhandler;

function errorhandler( msg, url, ln ){
alert("Error: "+msg+"\nIn File: "+url+"\nAt Line: "+ln);
return true;
}

// This is a deliberate mistake
document.form[ theMistake ].value = "myButton";
```

Document Properties

This chapter illustrates properties and methods of the window.document object. Image-swapping rollovers are demonstrated and cookies are explained. There is also an overview of how layers are used in JavaScript.

Covers

Chapter Ten

Set Colours

The properties and methods of the window.document object enable a web page document to be changed at runtime.

Using JavaScript to assign new values to properties of the window.document object causes the web browser to update the appearance of the web page in line with the new values.

This can be simply illustrated by assigning new values to the document.bgColor and document.fgColor properties to change the background and foreground colours of a page.

In this example the setcolor() function runs when the user pushes the button and the page appearance is changed:

```
function setcolor(){
window.document.bgColor = "black";
window.document.fgColor = "white";
}
```

JavaScript Creates

The write() method of the window.document object is a tremendously powerful feature that allows JavaScript to create content dynamically when loading a web page.

The method takes a single string argument containing the content to be written into the page and this may include html tags to format the content.

Using write() JavaScript can create browser-specific layers - see page 122.

Typically the document.write() method appears within a script block in the body section of an html document and will write selected content following a conditional test.

It should be noted that calling this method at runtime will cause the specified content to be written into a new blank document so replacing the current page.

Variable values may also be concatenated with a string argument in order to introduce a result assigned to a variable into the content of a web page.

This example first generates a random number then tests to determine if the number is odd or even. Selected content is added to the page depending on the result of this test:

```
var n, ntype;

n = Math.ceil( Math.random() * 100 );

ntype = ( n % 2 == 0 ) ? "Even" : "Odd";

document.write("<h1>Number " +n+ " is " +ntype+"</h1>");
```

Set Cookie

Cookies are tiny files that can be written by JavaScript to store small amounts of data on the local hard drive.

There are limitations to the use of cookies that restrict their size to 4 kilobytes and web browsers are not required to retain more than 20 cookies per web server.

Typically a cookie may often retain user data for use across web pages or on subsequent visits to a web site.

Escape the values to include spaces, commas and semicolons.

The cookie data is held in the window.document.cookie object as a name/value pair where the value may not contain any semicolons, commas or whitespace.

Multiple name/value pairs may be stored in a cookie by making further assignations to the document.cookie object.

The life-span of a cookie is limited to the length of the current browser session unless an expiry date is specified when the cookie is first set.

Expiration is assigned to a key named "expires" by amending a current date object to the desired future date.

Dates of expiry should be expressed in GMT string format by converting the amended date object using the date.toGMTString() method.

The calculation in the example below multiplies the days, hours, minutes, seconds and milliseconds to increment a date object by exactly 1 week.

This example stores the user's name and account number in a cookie with a life-span of 7 days:

A cookie may be deleted by setting an expiry date that is before the real current date.

```javascript
var useraccount = "Mike McGrath,000456";

var expiry = new Date();

expiry.setTime( expiry.getTime() + (7*24*60*60*1000) );

document.cookie = "cookiedata="+escape(useraccount)+";"

                + "expires=" +expiry.toGMTString()+ ";" ;
```

Get Cookie

If a cookie is set the document.cookie property will return true so JavaScript can test for the presence of cookies.

When a cookie is located the document.cookie property returns the stored data string.

Parts of the data may be retrieved from the stored string using the regular string manipulation methods covered earlier in this book.

Unescape any escaped data when retrieving from cookies.

The following script example is located in a different html document to the one on the facing page but both are in the same directory on the server.

As this second document is loaded into a web browser it first seeks the cookie set by the last example then extracts the data value to write customized dynamic content:

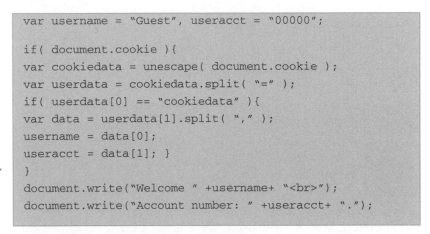

```
var username = "Guest", useracct = "00000";

if( document.cookie ){
var cookiedata = unescape( document.cookie );
var userdata = cookiedata.split( "=" );
if( userdata[0] == "cookiedata" ){
var data = userdata[1].split( "," );
username = data[0];
useracct = data[1]; }
}
document.write("Welcome " +username+ "<br>");
document.write("Account number: " +useracct+ ".");
```

Multiple name/ value pairs will automatically be returned with a semicolon separating each pair. Use string.indexOf() to identify the required pair.

Cookies - Microsoft Internet Explorer

File   Edit   View   Favorites   Tools   Help

Welcome Mike McGrath
Account number: 000456.

Images Array

The window.document.images[] object is an array of all image objects contained within a web page in the order in which the html code added them to the page.

So the first listed image is allocated to the first array element and can be addressed as document.images[0].

The name assigned by the html name attribute and the source url can be accessed for each image along with the total length of the images array. In the screenshot below the names displayed are those assigned in the html code:

Always give images a name with the html name attribute.

This example assumes these images appear in the html code from left to right, but this may not always be the case.

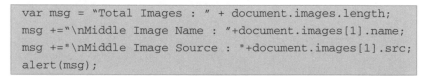

```
var msg = "Total Images : " + document.images.length;
msg +="\nMiddle Image Name : "+document.images[1].name;
msg +="\nMiddle Image Source : "+document.images[1].src;
alert(msg);
```

Rollover

If an image has been given a name in the html code, by assigning a value to the name attribute within the <img> tag, it may also be addressed by this name in JavaScript.

The syntax for this is document.images.imgname so that an image named "click" is addressed document.images.click.

Assigning a new value to the "src" property of an image at runtime causes the browser to replace the image in the page.

Typically this is seen in rollovers. When the user places the cursor over an image it is replaced by a second image, then the original image is returned when the cursor moves away.

The images array elements are only available after the browser has parsed the html code.

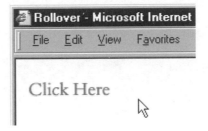 

The html <img> tag must be surrounded by an anchor tag to include calls to a JavaScript swapping function whenever the onmouseover or onmouseout events occur, as seen in this example of a simple rollover script:

Preload the swap image to avoid download delay (page 52) and only use images of like dimensions.

```
<SCRIPT TYPE = "text/javascript" >
<!--
function swap(n){
if( n == 0 )document.images.click.src = "off.gif";
if( n == 1 )document.images.click.src = "over.gif";
}
//-->
</SCRIPT>

<A HREF = "link.htm"
ONMOUSEOVER = "swap(1)" ONMOUSEOUT = "swap(0)" >

<IMG NAME = "click" SRC = "off.gif"
WIDTH = "108" HEIGHT = "24" ALT = "" BORDER = "0" > </A>
```

Dynamic Content

The window.document.open() method opens a new html document which can be written to using the familiar method window.document.write() to create dynamic content.

When the content has been written the document stream should be closed by the window.document.close() method.

The example below builds on the popup window example in the last chapter by writing the content from JavaScript instead of simply loading an existing html document:

Pass an empty string as the url argument to open an empty window.

```
function popup(){

var popwindow =
window.open("","","top=40,left=30,width=200,height=125");

popwindow.document.open();

popwindow.document.write("Dynamic JavaScript Page<p>");

popwindow.document.write
("<img src='welcome.gif' width='145' height='49'>");

popwindow.document.close();
}
```

Remember to use single quotes inside double quotes.

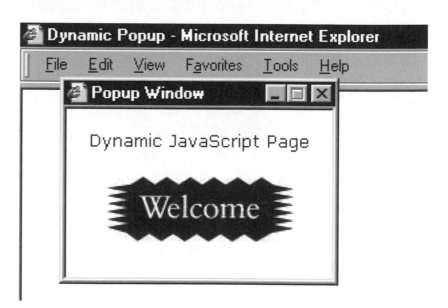

Last Modified

The window.document.lastModified object can provide date and time information of when a web page was last updated.

This data is usually supplied to document.lastModified from the http file header sent by the web server.

In some instances the web server may omit this information so document.lastModified will, in those cases, return 0.

Typically this data is used to indicate how recently a web page has been updated so that the user knows how current the information contained on that page may be.

Usually this information is displayed at the bottom of a page in a smaller font than the general page text.

The example that follows first tests that a date has been supplied to document.lastModified, then writes the data into the html document:

This script block would normally be included at the end of the html document body section.

```
<SCRIPT TYPE = "text/javascript" >
<!--

if( Date.parse( document.lastModified ) != 0 )

document.write
( "Page last updated: " + document.lastModified );

//-->
</SCRIPT>
```

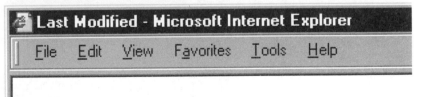

Internet Explorer Layers

JavaScript can create dynamic layers compatible with recent versions of Internet Explorer by using the document.write() method to write the html <div> tags with appropriate style attributes to supply property values.

This example creates two absolutely positioned layers:

```
document.write( " <div id = 'layer1'
style = ' position:absolute; top:20; left:20; width:150;
height:80; background-color:black; z-index:10 ' >
Layer #1 </div> " );

document.write( " <div id = 'layer2'
style = ' position:absolute; top:40; left:40; width:150;
height:80; background-color:silver; z-index:20 ' >
Layer #2 </div> " );
```

In Internet Explorer the layer's style object stores its properties.

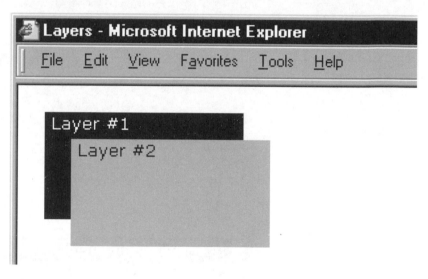

The script creates two objects, called in Internet Explorer window.layer1 and window.layer2, whose properties can be assigned new values to produce dynamic effect.

As window is the top level object it can be omitted from the address.

For example, to cause the black layer to be repositioned 100 pixels further right, a function could make this statement:

```
layer1.style.left = 120;
```

Netscape Layers

Netscape also recognises the <div> tag but only uses it for content blocks, not in z-index layers.

In a similar manner to the example on the facing page JavaScript creates dynamic layers compatible with recent versions of Netscape browsers using the document.write() method to write the html <layer> tags with appropriate attributes to supply property values.

The following example mirrors the Internet Explorer script to create two absolutely positioned layers in Netscape:

```
document.write( "<layer id = 'layer1' top ='20'
left ='20' width ='150' height = '80' bgColor = 'black'
z-index = '10' > Layer #1 </layer> " );

document.write( "<layer id = 'layer2' top ='40'
left ='40' width ='150' height = '80' bgColor = 'silver'
z-index = '20' > Layer #2 </layer> " );
```

In Netscape the layer object stores its own properties.

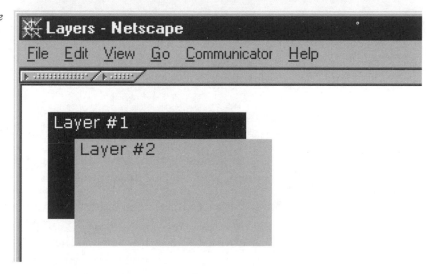

Netscape calls the two objects window.document.layer1 and window.document.layer2 whose properties can be assigned new values to produce dynamic effects.

For example, to cause the black layer to be repositioned 100 pixels further right, a function could make this statement:

```
document.layer1.left = 120;
```

Cross-Browser Layers

Strictly speaking there is no such thing as a cross-browser layer, only scripts that write layers compatible with the user's browser.

JavaScript can test for the existence of a document.all object to identify layer-capable Internet Explorer browsers.

Similarly the existence of a document.layers object will identify layer-capable Netscape browsers.

In the following example the script writes the appropriate layer for either of the above or displays an alert message.

```
if(document.all) document.write( "< div id = 'layer1'
style = 'position:absolute; top:20; left:20; width:80;
height:80; background-color:silver; z-index:10' > Layer
</div> " );

else if(document.layers) document.write( "<layer
id = 'layer1' top = '20' left = '20' width = '80' height
= '80' bgColor = 'silver' z-index = '10' > Layer
</layer> " );

else alert( navigator.appName + navigator.appVersion +
" cannot display DHTML content." );
```

In Internet Explorer any named html element can be addressed with document.all.elementname.

In addition to their usefulness in identifying browsers the document.all and document.layers objects have further uses.

Internet Explorer uses document.all object to store an array of all the html elements in a document. The object created in the above example for Internet Explorer is window.layer1 but this can also be addressed through the document.all array as window.document.all.layer1.

Netscape stores an array of all the layers in a document within the document.layers object. The object created in the above example for Netscape is window.document.layer1 but this can also be addressed through the document.layers array as window.document.layers.layer1.

Form Properties

This chapter illustrates how JavaScript can manipulate user input from html form elements. Examples are given for all common form input elements including radio buttons and selection boxes together with email address validation.

Covers

Chapter Eleven

The Form Object

The window.document.forms[] object contains an array of all the forms in an html document indexed in the order in which they appear in the html code.

For instance, window.document.forms[0] addresses the first form to appear in the html code of a web page.

If the name attribute of the <form> element has been assigned a value then the form can be addressed by name.

So a form named "f" can simply be addressed as document.f.

All other attributes assigned in the <form> tag are also accessible as properties of that form object.

The example below shows how JavaScript may refer to the properties of a typical html <form> element:

The enctype attribute value is stored by the property name "encoding".

This property is read-only but all other properties may be assigned new values.

```
<FORM NAME = "f" METHOD = "post"
ACTION = "mailto:a@b.com" ENCTYPE = "text/plain">

<SCRIPT TYPE = "text/javascript">
<!--
var msg = "Name: "    + document.f.name;
msg += "\nMethod: "   + document.f.method;
msg += "\nAction: "   + document.f.action;
msg += "\nEnctype: " + document.f.encoding;
alert(msg);
//-->
</SCRIPT>
```

Form Elements

The window.document.forms[].elements[] object contains an array of all the elements within a form indexed in the order in which they appear in the html code.

With a form named "f" for instance, document.f.elements[0] addresses the first element that appears in that form.

If the name attribute of the element has been assigned a value then the element can be addressed by name.

So an element named "btn1" in a form named "f" can simply be addressed as document.f.btn1.

Other attributes are accessible as properties of that element as illustrated by this example:

This example also uses a form named "f" although the <form> tags are not shown to save on space.

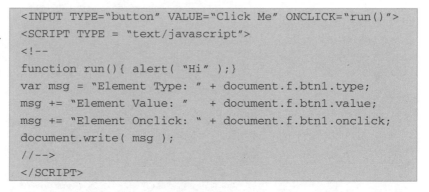

```
<INPUT TYPE="button" VALUE="Click Me" ONCLICK="run()">
<SCRIPT TYPE = "text/javascript">
<!--
function run(){ alert( "Hi" );}
var msg = "Element Type: " + document.f.btn1.type;
msg += "Element Value: "   + document.f.btn1.value;
msg += "Element Onclick: " + document.f.btn1.onclick;
document.write( msg );
//-->
</SCRIPT>
```

When the button in this example is pushed an alert dialog box will appear with a 'Hi' greeting.

Click Buttons

The values assigned in the html code may be reassigned by JavaScript so that a button will perform a different action.

In the example below an html onclick attribute specifies that the first() function will be called when the button is pushed.

The first() function assigns a string to a variable, then specifies a new eventhandler function called second() to the button's onclick attribute.

Subsequently pushing the button will call the second() function and execute the statement it contains.

When assigning eventhandler functions only assign the name, without any following brackets.

```
<FORM NAME = "f">
<INPUT TYPE = "button" NAME = "btn1" VALUE = "Click Me"
ONCLICK = "first()">  </FORM>

<SCRIPT TYPE = "text/javascript">
<!--
var msg;
function first(){
msg = "This message was left by the first function";
document.f.btn1.onclick = second;
}

function second(){
alert( "Hi, I'm the second function\n" + msg);
}

//-->
</SCRIPT>
```

Toggle Value

It is useful to change the label that is displayed on a button by the value attribute if that button performs dual actions.

In the following example a button, "btn1" in a form named "f", calls a stopgo() function to start and also stop a counter. The counter increments an integer variable at 1-second intervals and displays the count in the window's status bar.

The button label normally reads "Start " but changes to "Stop" if the timer count() function is running.

The num variable is initialized at -1 so that when first incremented the counter will start at zero.

The ! operator is used here to change the boolean variable to the opposite of its current value.

```
var running = false;
var num = -1;

function count(){
if(running){
num++;
window.status = "Seconds elapsed: " + num;
var tim = setTimeout( "count()", 1000 ); }
else{
num = -1;
clearTimeout( tim ); }
}

function stopgo(){
running = !running;
count();
document.f.btn1.value = (running)? "Stop" : "Start";
}
```

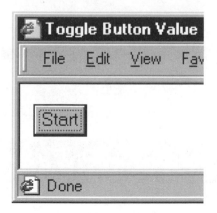

Text Boxes

The text displayed in an html text input is easily changed by JavaScript simply by assigning a new string to the value property of that form element.

Traditionally text boxes have been restricted to display text in just one fixed font but recent versions of Internet Explorer allow choice of font, style, size and colour.

The example below displays a string in a text box and adds style characteristics in recent Internet Explorer browsers:

Use a with statement to improve this code and avoid repetition of document.f.txt1.style.

```
<FORM NAME = "f" >
<INPUT TYPE = "text" NAME = "txt1" SIZE = "25 "> </FORM>

document.f.txt1.value = "JavaScript in easy steps";

if(document.all){
document.f.txt1.style.fontFamily = "comic sans ms";
document.f.txt1.style.fontSize = "16pt";
document.f.txt1.style.color = "white";
document.f.txt1.style.backgroundColor = "black";
}
```

The <script> tags are omitted from this example to save space.

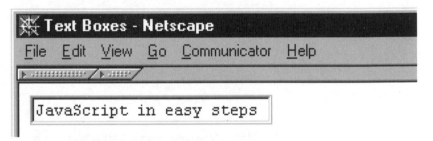

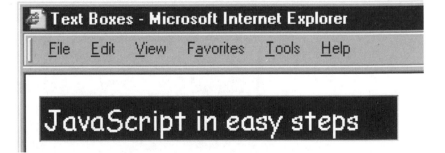

Password Boxes

A password input is simply another text box that displays asterisks in place of the actual characters.

The example below converts the actual string input to lower case then assigns the string to a variable.

If the variable string matches the correct password then the browser will load the first page of the website but will display an alert message if the string does not match.

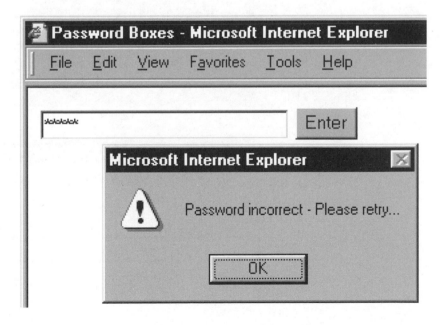

The final line in the script block will clear the password box after the user clicks the alert OK button, to be ready for another entry.

```
<FORM NAME = "f">
<INPUT TYPE = "password" NAME = "pwd1" SIZE = "25">
<INPUT TYPE = "button" NAME = "btn1" VALUE = "Enter"
ONCLICK = "validate()">
</FORM>

function validate(){
var entry = document.f.pwd1.value.toLowerCase();
if( entry == "admin" ) window.location = "page1.htm";
else{
alert( "Password incorrect - Please retry..." );
document.f.pwd1.value = ""; }
}
```

Radio Buttons

A group of radio buttons that will only allow one of the group to be checked at any time should all have the same name assigned to their name attribute in the <input> tag.

In the browser DOM the radio button group creates a document.form object with the given name.

This object contains an array of all radio buttons in the group with each one indexed in the order in which they appear in the html code.

JavaScript can address each radio button using the array name and index number. In the example below JavaScript checks the second radio button then displays both radio values in a text box:

Only checked radio buttons have their name/value pairs sent when the form is submitted.

```
<FORM NAME = "f">
<INPUT TYPE = "radio" NAME = "rad1" VALUE = "1">
<INPUT TYPE = "radio" NAME = "rad1" VALUE = "2">
<INPUT TYPE = "text"  NAME = "txt1" SIZE = "35">
</FORM>

<SCRIPT TYPE = "text/javascript">
<!--
document.f.rad1[1].checked = true;
var msg = "1st Radio Value: " +document.f.rad1[0].value;
msg += "   2nd Radio Value: " +document.f.rad1[1].value;
document.f.txt1.value = msg;
//-->
</SCRIPT>
```

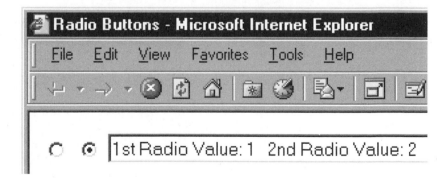

Radio Polling

The important feature of a radio button is wether it is checked or not. This can be ascertained from the radio button's checked property that will return a boolean true if the radio is checked or a boolean false if it is unchecked.

JavaScript can loop through all the radio button array elements to test for a true checked property, then use the value assigned to the radio button that is checked.

The example below illustrates how JavaScript finds a checked radio button and then uses its associated value:

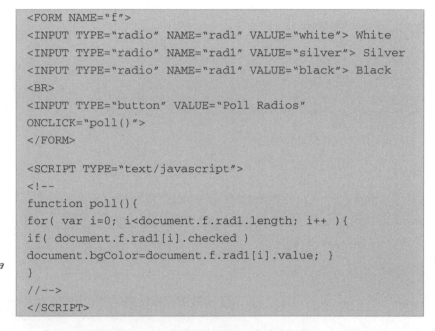

```
<FORM NAME="f">
<INPUT TYPE="radio" NAME="rad1" VALUE="white"> White
<INPUT TYPE="radio" NAME="rad1" VALUE="silver"> Silver
<INPUT TYPE="radio" NAME="rad1" VALUE="black"> Black
<BR>
<INPUT TYPE="button" VALUE="Poll Radios"
ONCLICK="poll()">
</FORM>

<SCRIPT TYPE="text/javascript">
<!--
function poll(){
for( var i=0; i<document.f.rad1.length; i++ ){
if( document.f.rad1[i].checked )
document.bgColor=document.f.rad1[i].value; }
}
//-->
</SCRIPT>
```

In JavaScript if(checked) is shorthand for a boolean test that in full would be if(checked==true).

Check Boxes

Unlike radio buttons a checkbox operates independently from other checkboxes and so all checkboxes should be uniquely named by their name attribute in the html code.

Each checkbox creates a document.form object with its given name and, like a radio button, has a checked property.

In the following example JavaScript sets the checked property of three checkboxes when the user pushes a button:

Only those checkboxes that are checked will have their name/value pairs sent on submission of the form to the server.

```
<FORM NAME="f">
<INPUT TYPE="checkbox" NAME="chk1" VALUE="details">
Send Details <BR>
<INPUT TYPE="checkbox" NAME="chk2" VALUE="samples">
Send Samples <BR>
<INPUT TYPE="checkbox" NAME="chk3" VALUE="catalog">
Send Catalogue <BR>
<INPUT TYPE="button" VALUE="Send Everything"
ONCLICK="checkall()"> <FORM>

<SCRIPT TYPE="text/javascript">
function checkall(){  with(document.f){
chk1.checked=true;
chk2.checked=true;
chk3.checked=true; }
}
</SCRIPT>
```

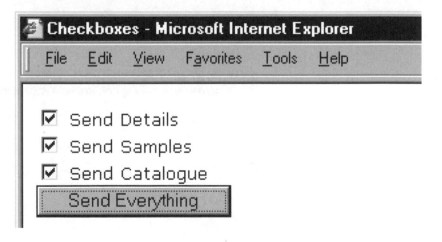

Checkbox Polling

The checked property of a checkbox object is most important and JavaScript may test for checked checkboxes then use their associated values.

The example below tests the checked property of all checkboxes and assigns the value of those that are checked to a string variable for display in an alert dialog box:

```
<FORM NAME="f">
<INPUT NAME="chk1" TYPE="checkbox" VALUE="Red"> Red<BR>
<INPUT NAME="chk2" TYPE="checkbox" VALUE="Green">
Green<BR>
<INPUT NAME="chk3" TYPE="checkbox" VALUE="Blue">
Blue<BR>
<INPUT TYPE="button" VALUE="Poll" ONCLICK="poll()">
</FORM>

function poll(){
var res = "Colour choice is ";
for( var i=1; i<4; i++ ){
if( eval( "document.f.chk" +i+ ".checked" ) )
res += eval( "document.f.chk" +i+ ".value+ ' ' "); }
alert( res ); }
```

Use eval() to combine form object names and numbers.

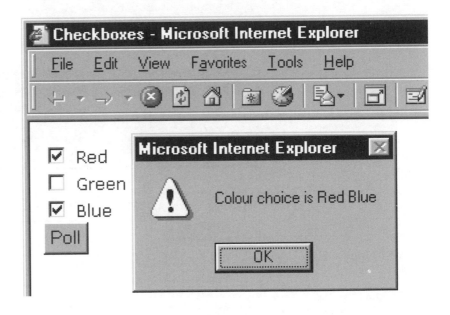

Option Lists

The items in an options list have a text property for the displayed string label and a value that is associated with the name of the select element when the item is selected.

This name/value pair is sent to the server when the form is submitted.

All menu items are stored in the object's options[] array and both the text label and its value may be dynamically written by JavaScript as illustrated by this example:

The options[] elements are initially created by html code.

```
<FORM NAME = "f">
<SELECT NAME = "s"><OPTION><OPTION><OPTION></SELECT>
<INPUT TYPE = "button" VALUE = "Set Options"
ONCLICK = "set()">                            </FORM>

<SCRIPT TYPE = "text/javascript">
<!--
function set(){
with( document.f.s ) {
options[0].text = "One"; options[0].value = "1";
options[1].text = "Two"; options[1].value = "2";
options[2].text = "Three"; options[2].value = "3"; }
}
//-->
</SCRIPT>
```

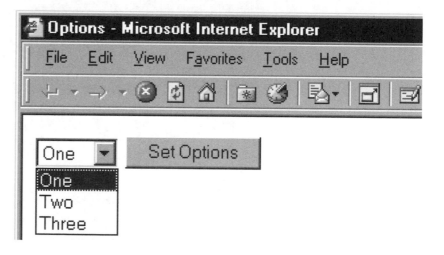

Selected Index

An options[] array has a property called selectedIndex that contains the index number of the item currently selected.

JavaScript can most usefully retrieve the value of the current selection for dynamic effects.

This example gets the value of the current selection for display in a text box:

```
<FORM NAME = "f">
<SELECT NAME = "s">
<OPTION VALUE = "apple">  Apple
<OPTION VALUE = "plum">   Plum
<OPTION VALUE = "orange"> Orange
</SELECT>
<INPUT TYPE = "button" VALUE = "Show Choice"
ONCLICK = "show()"> <BR>
<INPUT TYPE = "text" NAME = "txt1">
</FORM>

<SCRIPT TYPE = "text/javascript">
<!--
function show(){
var pick = document.f.s.selectedIndex;
document.f.txt1.value=document.f.s.options[pick].value;
}
//-->
</SCRIPT>
```

Use a with statement to make the script more concise.

Text Areas

A text area element is rather like a large scrolling text box input whose value can be read and written by JavaScript.

The example below writes content to a textarea by assigning a string to its value property when the document loads.

The function to assign the string is designated as the document's onload event handler by the script.

Care is needed when using this approach if the script is located in the <head> section of the document because the onload attribute of the html <body> tag may overwrite it.

 It is often best to call onload functions using the onload attribute of the html <body> element.

```
<SCRIPT TYPE = "text/javascript">
<!--

function dotext(){
document.f.txtarea1.value = "Welcome\nPlease read the
following notice carefully...";
}
window.onload = dotext;
//-->
</SCRIPT>

<FORM NAME = "f">
<TEXTAREA NAME = "txtarea1" ROWS = "3" COLS = "30">
</TEXTAREA>
</FORM>
```

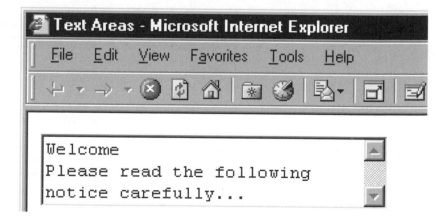

Clear Form

The reset() method of a form object will reset all the values within the form and update the inputs to their original state just as if the user had pushed a reset button.

See page 155 for an example of reset confirmation using the onreset event.

Careful use should be made of the reset() method to avoid the need for the user to input data repeatedly.

It is also advisable for the script to confirm the user's intention with the onreset event before resetting a form.

The example below uses the "javascript:" protocol to make a JavaScript function the target of a link enabling an image to reset the form when clicked in place of a reset button.

Short pieces of JavaScript can be inserted into a html document this way without the need for a script block:

Add attribute BORDER="0" to the image tag to remove the link border.

```
<FORM NAME="f">

<INPUT NAME="box1" TYPE="checkbox" VALUE="fun"> Fun JavaScript

<INPUT NAME="box2" TYPE="checkbox" VALUE="great"> Great JavaScript

<INPUT NAME="box3" TYPE="checkbox" VALUE="easy"> Easy JavaScript

</FORM>

<A HREF="javascript:document.f.reset()">
<IMG SRC="clear.jpg" WIDTH="205" HEIGHT="31" ALT=""></A>
```

See page 160 for more on the javascript: protocol.

Send Form

When a form is submitted to the server the values assigned to the name and value attributes of each form element are sent as name/value pairs.

The submit() method of the form object can be used to send the form to the server in exactly the same way as if the user had pushed a html submit button.

Like the example on the previous page this method can be used to replace a standard button with a graphic image that when clicked will call the JavaScript function.

See page 160 for more on the javascript: protocol.

The example below uses the "javascript:" protocol to make the JavaScript function a link target that will submit the form when the user clicks the link:

Add attribute BORDER="0" to the image tag to remove the link border.

```
<FORM NAME="f" METHOD="post" ACTION="mailto:a@b.com"
ENCTYPE="text/plain">

<INPUT NAME="box1" TYPE="checkbox" VALUE="fun"> Fun JavaScript
<INPUT NAME="box2" TYPE="checkbox" VALUE="great">Great JavaScript
<INPUT NAME="box3" TYPE="checkbox" VALUE="easy"> Easy JavaScript

</FORM>

<A HREF="javascript:document.f.submit()">
<IMG SRC="send.jpg" WIDTH="205" HEIGHT="31" ALT=""></A>
```

Amend Form

The onsubmit property of a form object can be used to call a JavaScript function when the user pushes a submit button.

This function will be executed then the form will be submitted to the server.

JavaScript can amend the form so that the name/value pairs can be better used by a receiving CGI script.

In the example below any empty text input has a zero value assigned by the function called with onsubmit:

The <script> tags are omitted from this example to save space.

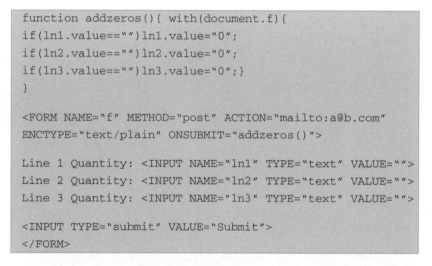

```
function addzeros(){ with(document.f){
if(ln1.value=="")ln1.value="0";
if(ln2.value=="")ln2.value="0";
if(ln3.value=="")ln3.value="0";}
}

<FORM NAME="f" METHOD="post" ACTION="mailto:a@b.com"
ENCTYPE="text/plain" ONSUBMIT="addzeros()">

Line 1 Quantity: <INPUT NAME="ln1" TYPE="text" VALUE="">
Line 2 Quantity: <INPUT NAME="ln2" TYPE="text" VALUE="">
Line 3 Quantity: <INPUT NAME="ln3" TYPE="text" VALUE="">

<INPUT TYPE="submit" VALUE="Submit">
</FORM>
```

The screenshot shows the user has entered a Line 1 quantity then clicked Submit which has added the zeros from JavaScript.

Email Address Validation

The value of form elements may be validated for correct format before the form is submitted.

In the following example JavaScript tests the format of a text input string for features of a valid email address and will only submit the form if the validation appears correct:

The example tests for the presence of "@" and "." characters that must be present in any valid email address. Further validation could be made of this input value and others before final submission.

```
<SCRIPT TYPE="text/javascript">
<!--
function send_if_valid(){ if(
document.f.email.value.indexOf("@")== -1 )
fail("No '@' in address");
else{
var adr = document.f.email.value.split("@");
if(adr[0].length < 1 ) fail("User address absent");
else if(adr[1].indexOf(".")== -1 ) fail("No dot");
else if(adr[1].length < 3 ) fail("Domain incorrect");
else document.f.submit(); }
}

function fail(msg){
alert("Email Address Error:\n" +msg); }
//-->
</SCRIPT>

<FORM NAME="f" METHOD="post" ACTION="mailto:a@b.com">
Enter Email Address...<BR>
<INPUT NAME="email" TYPE="text" VALUE="">
<INPUT TYPE="button" VALUE="Submit Form"
ONCLICK="send_if_valid()">
</FORM>
```

Event Handlers

User actions such as a key depression or a mouse click create events that JavaScript can use to interact with the user. This chapter describes common events and illustrates how they may be used by a JavaScript eventhandler.

Covers

Chapter Twelve

Mouse Click

The most common interactive event is the Click event created when a user clicks the left-hand mouse button while the cursor is over a form button in a web document.

An onclick eventhandler is normally assigned in the button's html <input> tag with the html onclick attribute.

Typically the value assigned to the html attribute will be a call to a JavaScript function that will execute statements.

This simple example calls a JavaScript function when the user clicks on a button and passes a string argument for use in the called function:

Put single quotes inside the double quotes used to assign a string.

```
<SCRIPT TYPE = "text/javascript" >
<!--

function doclick( str ){
document.f.txt.value = str;
}

//-->
</SCRIPT>

<FORM NAME = "f" >

<INPUT TYPE = "text" NAME = "txt" VALUE = "" >

<INPUT TYPE = "button" VALUE = "Do Click"
ONCLICK = "doclick( 'JavaScript in easy steps' )" >

</FORM>
```

Capture Mouse

It is extremely useful to know the whereabouts of the cursor when dealing with JavaScript in dhtml scripting.

Whenever the user moves the cursor a MouseMove event occurs and this can be captured by JavaScript for use with an onmousemove eventhandler.

The example below gives a useful way of determining x-y screen coordinates when developing dhtml scripts.

The MouseMove event is captured, then the onmousemove eventhandler dynamically displays the x-y coordinates:

 The first script statement in the example is to trap mouse movements in Netscape and capitalization must be exactly correct.

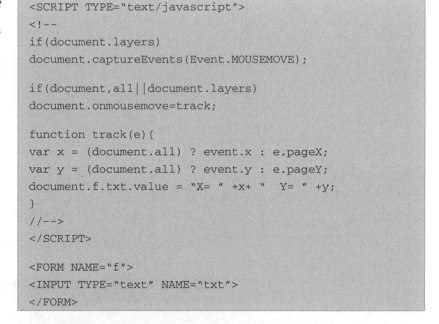

```
<SCRIPT TYPE="text/javascript">
<!--
if(document.layers)
document.captureEvents(Event.MOUSEMOVE);

if(document,all||document.layers)
document.onmousemove=track;

function track(e){
var x = (document.all) ? event.x : e.pageX;
var y = (document.all) ? event.y : e.pageY;
document.f.txt.value = "X= " +x+ "  Y= " +y;
}
//-->
</SCRIPT>

<FORM NAME="f">
<INPUT TYPE="text" NAME="txt">
</FORM>
```

 The Netscape and Internet Explorer DOM use different object names for the cursor's XY position.

Mouse Over

A MouseOver event occurs when the user places the cursor over a html hyperlink on a web page.

The anchor <a> and <area> tags can specify an eventhandler for the MouseOver event by assigning a JavaScript function call to their onmouseover html attribute.

Most frequently the eventhandler will perform an image swap as a rollover effect but any statements may be executed.

The example below assigns a string value to an input text box when the cursor is placed over an image:

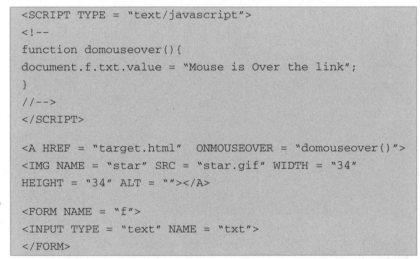

```
<SCRIPT TYPE = "text/javascript">
<!--
function domouseover(){
document.f.txt.value = "Mouse is Over the link";
}
//-->
</SCRIPT>

<A HREF = "target.html"  ONMOUSEOVER = "domouseover()">
<IMG NAME = "star" SRC = "star.gif" WIDTH = "34"
HEIGHT = "34" ALT = ""></A>

<FORM NAME = "f">
<INPUT TYPE = "text" NAME = "txt">
</FORM>
```

Although the ALT attribute contains just an empty string it should always be included in HTML 4.0.

Mouse Out

A MouseOut event occurs when the user moves the cursor away from a html hyperlink on a web page.

The anchor <a> and <area> tags can specify an eventhandler for the MouseOut event by assigning a JavaScript function call to their onmouseout html attribute.

Most frequently the eventhandler will perform an image swap to return an image to its original state in a rollover.

The following example builds on the previous example by adding an onmouseout eventhandler to change the value of a text box when the cursor moves off the link:

This example still uses a form named "f" containing a text input element named "txt".

```
<SCRIPT TYPE = "text/javascript">
<!--
function mousehandler(n){
with(document.f.txt){
if( n==1 ) value = "Mouse is Over the link";
if( n==0 ) value = "Mouse is Out of link area"; }
}
//-->
</SCRIPT>

<A HREF = "target.html"  ONMOUSEOVER = "mousehandler(1)"
ONMOUSEOUT = "mousehandler(0)">
<IMG NAME = "star" SRC = "star.gif" WIDTH = "34"
HEIGHT = "34" ALT = ""> </A>
```

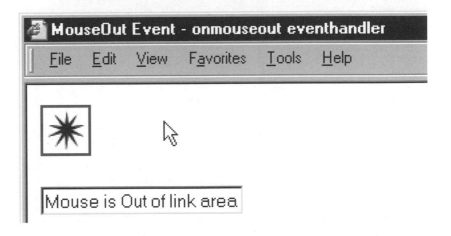

Mouse Down & Mouse Up

A MouseDown event occurs when the user presses a mouse button and a MouseUp event occurs when it is released.

Typically these are used together so that a single mouse click will use two eventhandlers.

This example swaps an image and changes the value of a text box when a mouse button is pressed but reverts both to their original state when the mouse button is released:

The document, link, image and button html elements all support attributes for onmouseup and onmousedown.

```
function light(n){
if( n == 1 ){
document.images.bulb.src = "bulbon.gif";
document.f.txt.value = "Mouse button is Down"; }
if( n == 0 ){
document.images.bulb.src = "bulboff.gif";
document.f.txt.value = "Mouse button is Up"; }
}

<IMG NAME = "bulb" SRC = "bulboff.gif" WIDTH = "72"
HEIGHT = "72" ALT = "">
<INPUT TYPE = "text" NAME = "txt" SIZE = "18">
<INPUT TYPE = "button" VALUE = "Light Switch"
ONMOUSEDOWN = "light(1)" ONMOUSEUP = "light(0)">
```

The <script> tags are omitted from this example to save space.

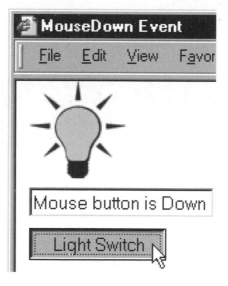

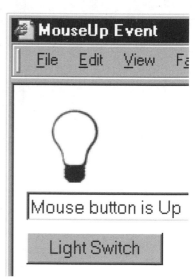

Mouse Buttons

JavaScript can determine which mouse button has been pressed by examining properties of the MouseDown event.

The left mouse button stores an integer value of one in the event.button property of Internet Explorer but this property is called e.which in Netscape and must be captured.

Here this property is used to inhibit the context menu that normally appears when the right mouse button is pressed:

Observe correct capitalization of the statement that captures MouseDown events in Netscape browsers.

```
<SCRIPT TYPE = "text/javascript">
<!--
var msg = "Right-Click Context Menu Is Disabled";

if( navigator.appName == "Netscape" )
window.captureEvents( Event.MOUSEDOWN );

function stopmenu(e){
if( navigator.appName == "Netscape" &&
( e.which == 2 || e.which == 3 )) {
alert( msg ); return false; }

if( navigator.appName == "Microsoft Internet Explorer"
&& ( event.button == 2 || event.button == 3 )) {
alert( msg ); return false; }
}
window.onmousedown = stopmenu;
document.onmousedown = stopmenu;

//-->
</SCRIPT>
```

Assign the eventhandler to onmousedown properties of both window and document objects to be cross-browser compliant.

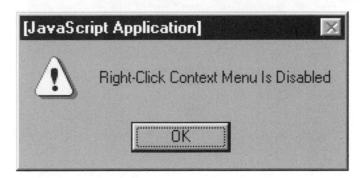

Key Down & Key Up

A KeyDown event occurs when the user presses a keyboard key button and a KeyUp event occurs when it is released.

Typically these are used together so that a single key depression will use two eventhandlers.

This example swaps an image and changes the value of a text box when a keyboard key button is pressed but reverts both to their original state when the mouse button is released:

```
if( navigator.appName == "Netscape" )
window.captureEvents( Event.KEYDOWN, Event.KEYUP );

function isdown(){
document.images.bulb.src = "bulbon.gif";
document.f.txt.value = "Key is Down";   }

function isup() {
document.images.bulb.src = "bulboff.gif";
document.f.txt.value = "Key is Up";       }

document.onkeydown = isdown; document.onkeyup = isup;

<IMG NAME = "bulb" SRC = "bulboff.gif" WIDTH = "72"
HEIGHT = "72" ALT = "">

<FORM NAME = "f">
<INPUT TYPE = "text" NAME = "txt" SIZE = "18"> </FORM>
```

The <script> tags are omitted from this example to save space.

Key Codes

The KeyDown event can also be used to get the character code of a key depression that is the Unicode reference number of that character key.

This example looks for the Y and N character codes, in both upper and lower case, then branches the script accordingly to assign a string value to a form text box:

Unicode values for common characters are the same as ASCII codes so in this example Y=89, N=78 y=121 and n=110.

```
<SCRIPT TYPE = "text/javascript">
<!--
if( document.layers )
window.captureEvents( Event.KEYDOWN );

function showkey(e){
var msg = "";
var fwd = "Y key pressed";
var hlt = "N key pressed";

if( navigator.appName == "Netscape" ) {
if( e.which == 89 || e.which == 121 ) msg = fwd;
if( e.which == 78 || e.which == 110)  msg = hlt;
}
if( navigator.appName == "Microsoft Internet Explorer"){
if( event.keyCode==89 || event.keyCode==121 ) msg = fwd;
if( event.keyCode==78 || event.keyCode==110 ) msg = hlt;
}
if( msg != "" ) document.f.txt.value = msg;
}

window.onkeydown=showkey;
document.onkeydown=showkey;
//-->
</SCRIPT>
```

Capture the KeyDown event and assign to both window and document eventhandlers for cross-browser compliancy.

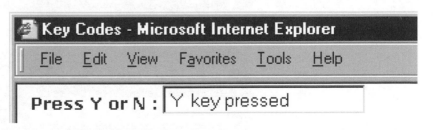

Load

The Load event does not occur until all the html elements on a web page have loaded so the onload eventhandler will only run after all elements are present on the page.

If a JavaScript in the document head section is to modify elements of the document body section the elements must already be loaded to avoid receiving a script error.

Typically the onload eventhandler will call a JavaScript function, often named init(), that will initialize a number of values on the page.

This example reverses the html page colours and assigns a value to a variable that it subsequently assigns to a text box:

A further eventhandler assigned to the onload attribute of the <body> tag would replace that assigned in the script.

```
<SCRIPT TYPE = "text/javascript">
<!--
function init(){
document.bgColor = "black";
document.fgColor = "white";
var str = "Page Loaded";
document.f.txt.value = str;
}
window.onload = init;
//-->
</SCRIPT>

<BODY BGCOLOR = "white" TEXT = "black">
<H2>Welcome...</H2>          <FORM NAME = "f">
<INPUT NAME = "txt" TYPE = "text" VALUE = "">
</FORM>
```

Unload

The Unload event occurs whenever the browser unloads a document from a window or frame, usually when the user navigates to a new url.

The onunload eventhandler may call a final JavaScript function to be run just before the document unloads.

When a frames page is unloaded the onunload eventhandler of each frame may call a final function.

The onunload eventhandler is useful to save the final state of data on that page in a cookie or by submission to the server.

It is also used to open new popup windows containing further information that the user may find useful.

The example below illustrates the use of the onunload eventhandler to open a new popup window:

The onunload eventhandler can also be assigned to the html onunload attribute in the <body> tag.

```
<SCRIPT TYPE = "text/javascript">
<!--
function finally(){

var win = window.open( "finally.htm", "",
"top=50,left=50,width=297,height=90" );
}

window.onunload = finally;

//-->
</SCRIPT>
```

Focus

The Focus event occurs when the user clicks on a form element or on a window to direct the browser's focus.

The onfocus eventhandler can call a JavaScript function when the focus is received.

In the example the string value of a textbox is replaced with an empty string when the user clicks on the text box:

Notice how the JavaScript 'this' keyword is used to pass the object reference of document.f.txt.

```
<FORM NAME = "f">
<INPUT NAME = "txt" TYPE = "text" VALUE = "Enter data
here" ONFOCUS = "this.value = '' "> </FORM>
```

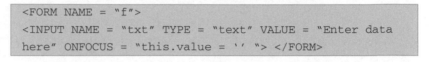

The focus() method of a form element is useful to move the cursor to the next required input position.

In this example if the value passed by the caller is not a number the text box is assigned an empty string and the cursor returns to the text box:

The isNaN() JavaScript function will evaluate an argument and return true if it is a number.

```
<SCRIPT TYPE = "text/javascript">
<!--
function examine( val ){
if ( isNaN( val ) ){
document.f.txt.value = ""; document.f.txt.focus(); }
}
//-->
</SCRIPT>
<FORM NAME = "f">
<INPUT NAME = "txt" TYPE = "text" VALUE = ""
ONCLICK = "examine( this.value )">
</FORM>
```

Blur

A Blur event occurs when the browser's focus moves away from a form element or a window and the onblur eventhandler may then call a JavaScript function.

In the following example the user is reminded that the text box they have just left should receive some input:

```
function isentry( val ){
if ( val == "" ){
alert( "Please enter data" ); document.f.txt.focus(); }
}
<FORM NAME = "f">
<INPUT NAME = "txt" TYPE = "text" VALUE = ""
ONBLUR = "isentry( this.value )">        </FORM>
```

Using the window.blur() method will minimize the window.

The blur() method of a form element is useful to prevent user input for text boxes that must be read-only.

This example blurs focus away from a text input if the user attempts to input:

```
<INPUT TYPE="text" VALUE="Read" ONFOCUS="blur(this)"
```

Change

The Change event occurs when the value of a text input is changed or when the user selects an item in an options list.

The onchange eventhandler can call a JavaScript function to execute some code whenever the Change event occurs.

The example below sets the initial selected option to green then assigns an eventhandler that displays the associated value in a text box whenever the selection is changed:

The <script> tags are omitted from this example to save space.

```
function init(){
document.f.s.options[1].selected = true;
document.f.s.onchange = showselected;
}
function showselected(){
document.f.txt.value =
document.f.s.options[document.f.s.selectedIndex].value;
}
window.onload = init;

<FORM NAME = "f">
<INPUT NAME = "txt" VALUE = "">
<SELECT NAME = "s">
<OPTION VALUE = "red">Red
<OPTION VALUE = "green">Green
<OPTION VALUE = "blue">Blue
</SELECT>
</FORM>
```

Reset

The Reset event occurs when the user pushes a form's reset button or when JavaScript executes the form.reset() method.

The onreset eventhandler may call a JavaScript function when the Reset event occurs.

In this example the eventhandler is assigned to the html onreset attribute in the <form> tag so that a radio value will be changed and its value displayed in a text box of a second form when the first form is reset.

The first radio button could be checked with JavaScript by assigning true to the property document.f1.r[0].checked.

```
<SCRIPT TYPE = "text/javascript">
<!--
function showvalue(){
document.f1.r[0].value = "Salmon";
document.f2.txt.value = document.f1.r[0].value;
}
//-->
</SCRIPT>

<FORM NAME = "f1" ONRESET = "showvalue()">
<INPUT TYPE= "radio" NAME= "r" VALUE= "Red" CHECKED>Red
<INPUT TYPE = "radio" NAME = "r" VALUE = "Green"> Green
<INPUT TYPE = "radio" NAME = "r" VALUE = "Blue">Blue
<INPUT TYPE = "reset" VALUE = "Reset">
</FORM>

<FORM NAME = "f2">
<INPUT TYPE = "text" NAME = "txt" VALUE = "">
</FORM>
```

Submit

The Submit event occurs when the user pushes a submit button in a form and the onsubmit eventhandler may call a function to ensure form validation before submission.

The onsubmit eventhandler is not invoked by use of the form.submit() method in JavaScript.

If the onsubmit eventhandler returns false, for instance when form validation fails, the form data will not be sent.

This example performs basic email address validation and provides the user with an alert message if validation fails:

```
function validation(){
if( document.f.email.value.indexOf( "@" ) == -1 ){
alert( "Email address is absent or incorrect" );
return false; }
}

<FORM NAME= "f" METHOD= "post" ACTION= "mailto:a@b.com"
ENCTYPE= "text/plain" ONSUBMIT= "return validation()">
Enter your email address:
<INPUT NAME = "email" TYPE = "text" VALUE = "">
<INPUT TYPE = "submit" VALUE = "Submit">
</FORM>
```

The <script> tags are omitted from this example to save space.

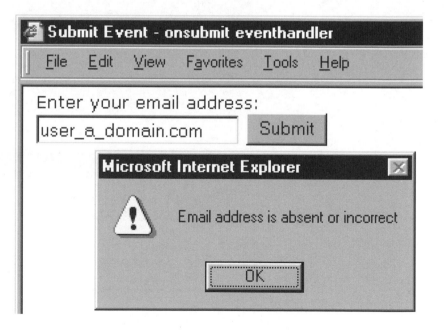

Abort

The Abort event occurs when the user cancels the download of an image, usually by pushing the stop button on a web browser's toolbar.

The onabort eventhandler may call a JavaScript function when an image download is cancelled.

Typically the eventhandler is assigned to the onabort attribute of the html <img> tag.

In the example below the eventhandler directly creates an alert message confirming that the download is cancelled:

One-line code statements can be assigned directly to the event handler - ONABORT="alert('message')".

```
<SCRIPT TYPE = "text/javascript">
<!--
function abortmsg(){
alert( "Image Download Aborted" );
}
//-->
</SCRIPT>
<IMG SRC = "bigpic.jpg" WIDTH = "1024" HEIGHT = "768"
ALT ="" ONABORT = "abortmsg()">
```

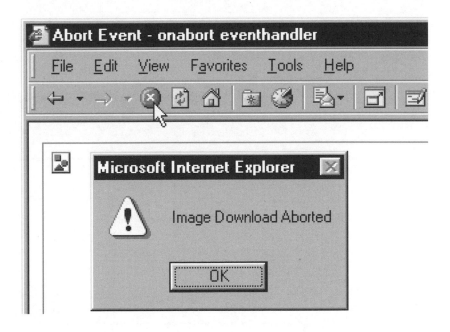

Resize

The Resize event occurs when a browser window is re-sized by the user and the onresize eventhandler can execute code to make the page appropriate for the new window size.

This is most useful to reposition dhtml page components as illustrated in the following example that creates a centred layer which will be re-centred if the window is re-sized:

The fixpos() function divides the window width by two to establish the window's horizontal centre. Now half of the layer's width is subtracted to determine the left position of the layer.

```
if( document.layers ) document.write( "<LAYER ID = 'lyr'
TOP = '20' BGCOLOR = 'silver' WIDTH = '100'
HEIGHT = '50' Z-INDEX = '10' > Layer </LAYER> ");

if( document.all ) document.write( "<DIV ID = 'lyr'
STYLE = 'position: absolute; top: 20px; width: 100;
height: 50px; background-color: silver;
z-index: 10'> Layer </DIV> ");

function fixpos(){
var innerwidth = ( document.layers ) ? self.innerWidth :
document.body.clientWidth;
var fixleft = ( innerwidth / 2 ) - 50;
( document.layers ) ? document.lyr.left = fixleft :
lyr.style.left = fixleft;
}
fixpos();
window.onresize = fixpos;
```

JavaScript in DHTML

This chapter describes the use of JavaScript to control and manipulate components of a html document. The many examples illustrate how characteristics of position, content and visibility can all be dynamically changed to create an exciting interactive web page.

Covers

Chapter Thirteen

JavaScript: Protocol

The javascript: protocol may be assigned to the href attribute in an html anchor element to make a JavaScript function the target of a hyperlink.

The name of the function should follow the protocol specifier to identify the script code to be executed or short pieces of code can be included in-line after the specifier.

The example below contains both in-line code and a function call, each will run when the users clicks their link:

To make an anchor that has no target use javascript:// so that other attributes like onmouseover can still be used.

```
<SCRIPT TYPE = "text/javascript">
<!--
function respond(){
alert("Script-block code");
}
//-->
</SCRIPT>
<A HREF="javascript:alert('In-line code')"> Link #1 </A>
<A HREF="javascript:respond()"> Link #2 </A>
```

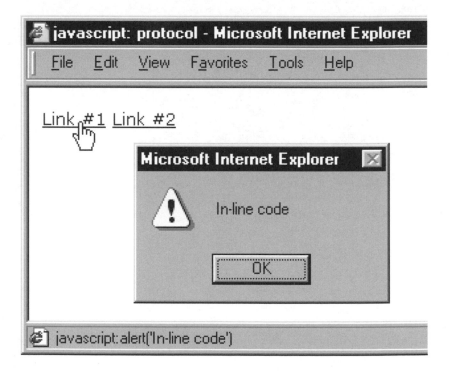

Layer Attributes

The six most important layer attributes to be used in dhtml are id, top, left, z-index, visibility and bgColor.

Also width and height attributes suggest an initial size for the layer but these may be adjusted to suit the layer's content and should not be changed dynamically.

In Netscape browsers these attributes are used in the <layer> tag to specify the characteristics of the layer and create properties of the layer object. So the position from the window top of a layer named "lyr" is document.lyr.top.

There are significant differences with Microsoft browsers as they use the style attribute in a <div> tag to assign the characteristics as a semi-colon delimited list. The position from the window top of a layer named "lyr" is lyr.style.top.

This example creates a layer and lists the value of the layer's top and left characteristics:

The attribute for the colour of the layer background in Internet Explorer is called background-color rather than bgColor.

```
if( document.layers ){
document.write( '<LAYER ID="lyr" top="15" left="170"
width="50" height="50" z-index="10" bgColor="silver"
visibility="visible">Layer</LAYER>' );
document.write( "Top=" + document.lyr.top +  "Left=" +
document.lyr.left ); }

if( document.all ){
document.write( '<DIV ID="lyr" STYLE="position:absolute;
top:15; left:170; width:50; height:50; z-index:10;
background-color:silver; visibility:visible">
Layer</DIV>' );
document.write( "Top=" + document.all.lyr.style.top +
"Left=" + document.all.lyr.style.left );
}
```

Internet Explorer needs the position to be specified as absolute to ensure correct positioning.

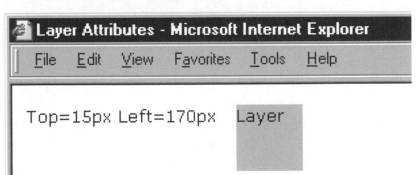

Toggle Visibility

Having determined how to create layers with JavaScript for both Netscape and Internet Explorer it's easy to have some fun with them by letting the JavaScript dynamically change their attribute values.

For example, changing the visibility attribute value to "hidden" will cause a layer to disappear from view.

Conversely a layer initially created with a visibility attribute value of "hidden" can be revealed by changing that value to "visible".

The following script toggles the visibility of a single layer with an onmouseover and onmouseout eventhandler but could easily toggle several layers for even greater effect:

The layer will not be written for older browsers that do not have dhtml capabilities.

```
<SCRIPT TYPE = "text/javascript">
<!--
if( document.layers ){
document.write( '<LAYER ID="lyr" top="15" left="100"
width="140" height="140" z-index="10"
visibility="hidden"><IMG SRC="apple.gif" WIDTH="140"
HEIGHT="140" BORDER="0"></LAYER>' );
}
if( document.all ){
document.write( '<DIV ID="lyr" STYLE="position:absolute;
top:15; left:100; width:50; height:50; z-index:10;
visibility:hidden"> <IMG SRC="apple.gif" WIDTH="140"
HEIGHT="140" BORDER="0"></DIV>' );                      }

function showapple(){
if(document.layers) document.lyr.visibility= "visible";
if(document.all) lyr.style.visibility= "visible";
}

function hideapple(){
if(document.layers) document.lyr.visibilty= "hidden";
if(document.all) lyr.style.visibility= "hidden";
}
//-->
</SCRIPT>
```

And the code for the html link looks like this:

```
<A HREF="javascript://" ONMOUSEOVER="showapple()"
ONMOUSEOUT="hideapple()"> Apple Link </A>
```

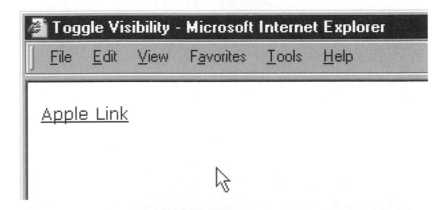

The javascript: protocol specifier will appear in the status bar in place of a target url address.

Dynamic Content

JavaScript can write content onto a layer it has created without affecting the contents elsewhere on the page.

The position of the layer will remain unaltered but the height of the layer will be automatically increased if the content will not fit into the existing layer size.

Also text will automatically wrap intelligently at the layer border so words will not be split.

The JavaScript example for this feature will create a layer, then dynamically write the text entered by the user into the text box when the user pushes the input button.

Notice the syntax for Netscape browsers where the document layer has itself got a document property.

JavaScripts that write layers should have their script block in the body of the document.

```
<SCRIPT TYPE = "text/javascript">
<!--
if( document.layers ){
document.write( '<LAYER ID="lyr" top="90" left="10"
width="200" height="20" z-index="10" bgColor="silver">
</LAYER>' );
}

if( document.all ){
document.write( '<DIV ID="lyr" STYLE="position:absolute;
top:90; left:10; width:200; height:20; z-index:10;
background-color:silver"> </DIV>' );
}

function write_entry(){
var str=document.f.txt.value;
if( document.all ) lyr.innerHTML=str;
if( document.layers ){
document.lyr.document.open();
document.lyr.document.write(str);
document.lyr.document.close(); }
}
//-->
</SCRIPT>
```

And the html code for the form looks like this:

```
Please enter some text below:
<FORM NAME="f">
<INPUT TYPE="text" VALUE="" NAME="txt">
<INPUT TYPE="button" VALUE="Write Entry"
ONCLICK="write_entry()">
</FORM>
```

Although this example uses text from user input JavaScript could write layer content from any function call.

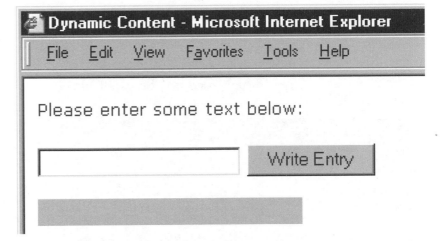

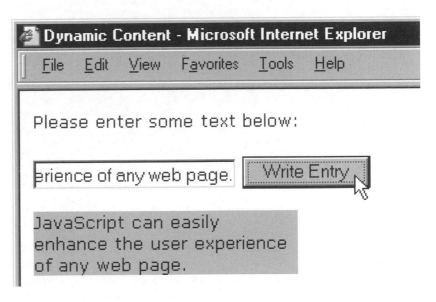

Slide Show

JavaScript can rotate images to create an automatic slide show that will update the current image after a predetermined interval.

In this script a preload routine first downloads all the images into the browser's cache to be readily available for display.

Rotation speed in milliseconds is specified by the value assigned to the variable named pause.

The variable named "n" is a counter that is incremented by the rotate() timer function and is used to display the image at that index number in the imgs[] array.

It is important that all the images should have the same dimensions and be small file sizes to avoid download delays.

Simply adding more image filenames to the imgs[] array will extend the slide show without further coding.

```
<SCRIPT TYPE = "text/javascript">
<!--

var pause = 3000;

var n = 0;

var imgs = new Array ( "butterfly.gif", "globe.gif",
"fish.gif", "clock.gif" );

var preload = new Array();
for( var i = 1; i < imgs.length; i++ ){
preload[i] = new Image();
preload[i].src = imgs[i];
}

function rotate(){
document.images.pic.src = imgs[n];
( n == (imgs.length - 1 )) ? n = 0 : n++;
setTimeout( "rotate()", pause );
}

window.onload = rotate;

// -->
</SCRIPT>
```

The html code used with the JavaScript slide show assigns the name "pic" to the original image so the script may address the image object as document.images.pic:

```
Enjoy the show<BR>

<IMG NAME = "pic" SRC = "bfly.gif" WIDTH = "72"
HEIGHT = "72" ALT = "" VSPACE = "5" HSPACE = "10">
```

 Ensure that all images are the actual size to be displayed so that the browser does not need to re-size them when displaying.

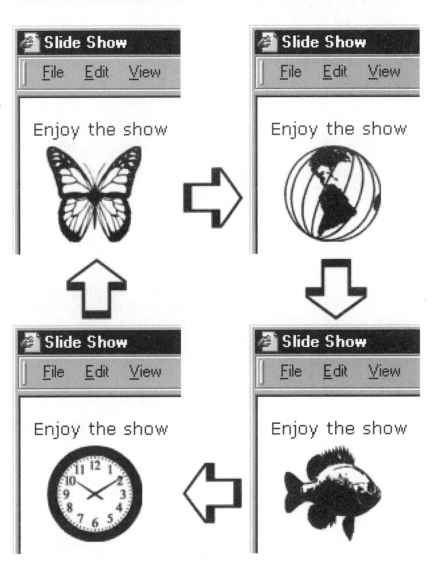

Tacking Layer

The left coordinate of a layer can be modified by JavaScript to reposition the layer along the X axis.

The following example writes a layer containing a sailboat image just outside the left edge of the window. Then a timer function sails the boat gracefully across the screen.

When the boat disappears off the right edge of the window JavaScript swaps the image for a pre-loaded version of the sailboat image facing in the opposite direction. The script then sails it back across the screen from right to left.

When the boat disappears off the left edge of the window the image reverts to the original version that proceeds to sail left to right and the boat continues to tack back and forth.

The "goright" variable determines the direction of travel. It's initially set to true but it is reversed at each extreme point.

The setsail() function can be viewed in two halves were the first half runs code for Internet Explorer while the second half runs Netscape code. This is a fine illustration of cross-browser JavaScript code that achieves the same effect in each browser but is simply ignored by other browsers.

Use animated gifs with this script to create even more exciting results.

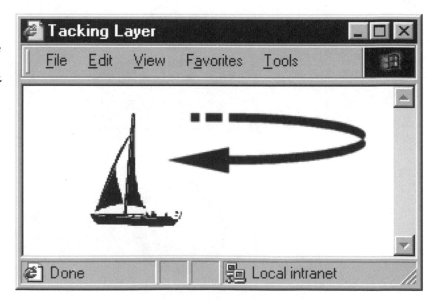

The <script> tags are omitted from this example to save space.

The positional pixel values in Internet Explorer have "px" tacked on the end (eg: left="70px") so the parseInt() method is needed to extract the integer part for manipulation.

JavaScript that writes layers should be located in the body of the html document.

```javascript
var preload = new Image(); preload.src = "sail_1.gif";
var goright = true;

if( document.all ) document.write( "<div id='boat'
style='position:absolute; top:20; left:-75; width:70;
height:85' ><img name='boat_image' src='sail_r.gif'
alt=''></div>" );

if( document.layers )document.write( "<layer id='boat'
top='20' left='-75' width='70' height='85'><img
name='boat_image' src='sail_r.gif' alt=''></layer>" );

function setsail(){
if( document.all ) {  if( goright )
boat.style.left = ( parseInt ( boat.style.left ) + 1 );
else boat.style.left = (parseInt(boat.style.left) - 1);

if( parseInt( boat.style.left ) >=
( document.body.clientWidth + 5 ) ) {
goright=false;
document.images.boat_image.src = "sail_1.gif"; }

if( parseInt ( boat.style.left ) <= -75 ) {
goright = true;
document.boat_image.src = "sail_r.gif"; }
}

if(document.layers){ if( goright )
document.boat.left += 1;
else document.boat.left -=1;

if( document.boat.left >= ( window.innerWidth + 5 ) ){
goright = false;
document.boat_image.src = "sail_1.gif"; }

if( document.boat.left <= -75 ){
goright = true;
document.boat_image.src = "sail_r.gif"; }
}

window.setTimeout( "setsail()", 50 );
}

setsail();
```

Scrolling Layer

Where the previous example modified the left property of the layer attribute, this example manipulates the layer's top property to move a layer higher or lower on the Y axis.

The script first creates a browser-specific layer that contains a simple helicopter image.

Html code adds rollover hyperlinks that call JavaScript functions but have a void link target url.

When the user places the cursor over the hyperlink called "Soar" a timer function increments the value of the top property so the layer moves higher in the window.

Placing the cursor over the hyperlink called "Sink" has the opposite effect and lowers the layer in the window.

In each case the timer function is cancelled when the cursor moves away from the hyperlink and the movement of the layer is discontinued.

Keeping the cursor over the "Soar" link will cause the image to go off the top of the window. A conditional limiter could be added to prevent this.

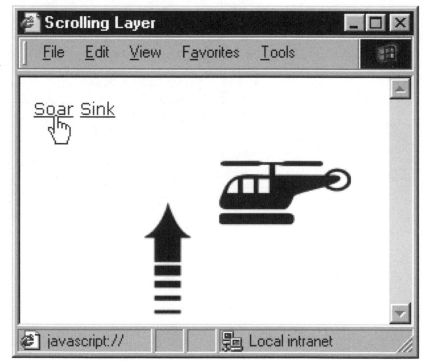

```
<SCRIPT TYPE = "text/javascript">
<!--

var timer;
var content = '<IMG SRC = "copter.gif" WIDTH = "100"
HEIGHT = "50" ALT = ""> ';

if(document.layers){
document.write('<LAYER ID = "lyr" top = "100"
left = "150">' + content + '</LAYER>' ); }

if(document.all){
document.write('<DIV ID="lyr" STYLE="position:absolute;
top:100; left:150">' + content + '</DIV>' ); }

function soar(){
if(document.all)lyr.style.top=parseInt(lyr.style.top)-1;
if(document.layers)document.lyr.top -=1;
timer = setTimeout( "soar()", 50);
}

function sink(){
if(document.all)lyr.style.top=parseInt(lyr.style.top)+1;
if(document.layers)document.lyr.top +=1;
timer=setTimeout( "sink()", 50);
}

function stop(){
clearTimeout(timer);
}

//-->
</SCRIPT>
```

The parseInt() method is needed to extract the layer's top value with Internet Explorer.

Change the timer delay from 50 to adjust the speed of scroll.

And the html code for the rollovers looks like this:

```
<A HREF = "javascript://" ONMOUSEOVER = "soar()"
ONMOUSEOUT = "stop()">Soar</A>

<A HREF = "javascript://" ONMOUSEOVER = "sink()"
ONMOUSEOUT = "stop()">Sink</A>
```

Pop-Up Layers

This example builds on the toggle visibility example given earlier in this chapter by writing multiple browser-specific layers which have their visibility toggled by an image map.

When the cursor is placed over an image map hyperlink, the JavaScript function will display the appropriate layer but will hide that layer when the cursor moves off the link.

Here is the html code for the image map that is used with the JavaScript code on the facing page:

```
<MAP NAME = "harsal">
<AREA SHAPE = RECT COORDS = "0,0,60,100"
HREF = "javascript://"  ALT = "" ONMOUSEOVER = "talk(0)"
ONMOUSEOUT = "hush(0)" >
<AREA SHAPE = RECT COORDS = "130,0,190,100"
HREF = "javascript://"  ALT = "" ONMOUSEOVER = "talk(1)"
ONMOUSEOUT = "hush(1)" >
</MAP>
```

This type of dynamic script can be used to great effect with navigation menu item rollovers.

```
<SCRIPT TYPE = "text/javascript">
<!--
var bod = '<IMG SRC= "harsal.gif" WIDTH= "190"
HEIGHT="100" USEMAP="#harsal" BORDER="0">';
var sal='<IMG SRC="hisal.gif" WIDTH="100" HEIGHT="40">';
var har='<IMG SRC="hihar.gif" WIDTH="100" HEIGHT="40">';

if(document.layers){
document.write('<LAYER ID="lyr" top= "80" left= "50">'
+ bod + '</LAYER> <LAYER ID="sal" top= "30" left= "130"
z-index= "10" visibility= "hidden">' + sal + '</LAYER>
<LAYER ID="har" top= "30" left= "55" z-index= "20"
visibility= "hidden">' + har + '</LAYER>'); }

if(document.all){
document.write('<DIV ID="lyr" STYLE= "position:absolute;
top:70; left:30" >' + bod + '</DIV> <DIV ID= "sal"
STYLE="position:absolute; top: 20; left:110; z-index:10;
visibility:hidden">' + sal + '</DIV> <DIV ID= "har"
STYLE= "position:absolute; top: 20; left:35; z-index:20;
visibility:hidden" >' + har + '</DIV>'); }

function talk(n){
if(document.all){
if(n==0)document.all.har.style.visibility= "visible";
if(n==1)document.all.sal.style.visibility= "visible"; }
if(document.layers){
if(n==0)document.har.visibility= "visible";
if(n==1)document.sal.visibility= "visible"; }
}

function hush(n){
if(document.all){
if(n==0)document.all.har.style.visibility= "hidden";
if(n==1)document.all.sal.style.visibility= "hidden"; }
if(document.layers){
if(n==0)document.har.visibility= "hidden";
if(n==1)document.sal.visibility= "hidden"; }
}

//-->
</SCRIPT>
```

Make the layers z-index values different if the layers overlap.

Always leave an area blank for onmouseout events to fire before having another onmouseover event.

Dynamic Menu

This example uses the mouse coordinates to toggle the visibility of menu layers and uses a style sheet to specify the characteristics of the main bar layer and the menu layers:

The layer syntax is assigned to variables which are later used by eval() to apply the code so enabling the script to be more concise.

```
<SCRIPT TYPE= "text/javascript">
<!--
if(document.layers)document.captureEvents(Event.MOUSEMOVE);
document.onmousemove = track;
divref = (document.all) ? "" : "document.";
stlref = (document.all) ? "style." : "";

function track(e){
var x = (document.all) ? event.x : e.pageX;
var y = (document.all) ? event.y : e.pageY;
if( x<1 || x>65 || y<53 || y>123 )
eval( divref + "b." + stlref + "visibility = 'hidden'");
if( x<80 || x>145 || y<53 || y>123 )
eval( divref + "c." + stlref + "visibility = 'hidden'");
if( x<160 || x>225 || y<53 || y>123 )
eval( divref + "d." + stlref + "visibility = 'hidden'");
}

function reveal(menu){
eval( divref + menu + "." + stlref + "visibility =
'visible'");      }
//-->
</SCRIPT>

<STYLE TYPE= "text/css">
<!--
.bar{ position:absolute; left:0; top:50; color:black;
width:800; height:20px; background:silver; font-
family:verdana; font-size:10pt; border-color:white;
border-width:1; }

.menu{ position:absolute; width:65; height:50;
background:silver; top:71px; visibility:hidden; font-
family:verdana; font-size:10pt; border-color:white;
border-width:1px; }
//-->
</STYLE>
```

Remember to capture the MouseMove event for Netscape users.

And the html code for this example looks like this:

Fix the font height to prevent changes in the browser font settings disrupting layers.

```
<DIV ID= "a" CLASS= "bar">
<A HREF="javascript://" ONMOUSEOVER="reveal('b')"> 
Menu 1</A> |
<A HREF="javascript://" ONMOUSEOVER="reveal('c')"> 
Menu 2</A>    |
<A HREF="javascript://" ONMOUSEOVER="reveal('d')"> 
Menu 3</A>    |
</DIV>

<DIV ID= "b" CLASS= "menu" STYLE= "left:0" LEFT= "0">
<A HREF= "target1.htm"> Item 1 </A>
<A HREF= "target2.htm"> Item 2 </A>
<A HREF= "target3.htm"> Item 3 </A> </DIV>

<DIV ID= "c" CLASS= "menu" STYLE= "left:80" LEFT= "80">
<A HREF= "target4.htm"> Item 1 </A>
<A HREF= "target5.htm"> Item 2 </A>
<A HREF= "target6.htm"> Item 3 </A> </DIV>

<DIV ID= "d" CLASS= "menu" STYLE= "left:160" LEFT="160">
<A HREF= "target7.htm"> Item 1 </A>
<A HREF= "target8.htm"> Item 2 </A>
<A HREF= "target9.htm"> Item 3 </A> </DIV>
```

Different width of menu heading and menu item descriptions will require changes to the coordinates in this example.

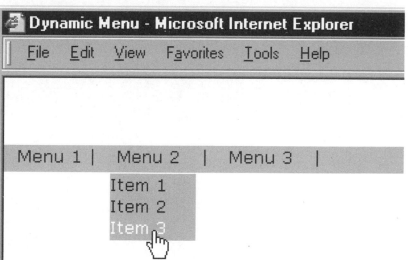

Fresh Options

In this example JavaScript dynamically changes menu options and their associated values depending on which radio button is checked:

```
<SCRIPT TYPE= "text/javascript">
<!--
function setcities(){
if( document.f.rad[0].checked ) jap();
if( document.f.rad[1].checked ) usa();
}

function jap(){
with( document.f.s.options[0] ){
selected=true; text="Select City..."; value=""; }
with(document.f.s.options[1]){
text="Kyoto"; value="kyoto"; }
with(document.f.s.options[2]){
text="Osaka"; value="osaka"; }
with(document.f.s.options[3]){
text="Tokyo"; value="tokyo"; }
showvalue();
}

function usa(){
with( document.f.s.options[0] ){
selected=true; text="Select City..."; value=""; }
with( document.f.s.options[1] ){
text="New York"; value="new york"; }
with( document.f.s.options[2] ){
text="Los Angeles"; value="los angeles"; }
with( document.f.s.options[3] ){
text= "Washington"; value="washington"; }
showvalue();
}

function showvalue(){
document.f.txt.value=
document.f.s.options[document.f.s.selectedIndex].value;
}
// -->
</SCRIPT>
```

The value of the selected option is displayed in the text box just for demonstration purposes.

The JavaScript can manipulate the options created in the html code but does not create new options.

```
<FORM NAME= "f">
Selected Value:<BR>
<INPUT TYPE="text" NAME="txt" VALUE="" SIZE="16"> <BR>
<INPUT TYPE="radio" NAME="rad" ONCLICK="setcities()">
Japan
<INPUT TYPE="radio" NAME="rad" ONCLICK="setcities()">
USA
<BR>
<SELECT NAME= "s" ONCHANGE= "showvalue()">
<OPTION VALUE="" SELECTED>Select Country...</OPTION>
<OPTION VALUE=""></OPTION>
<OPTION VALUE=""></OPTION>
<OPTION VALUE=""></OPTION>
</SELECT>
</FORM>
```

This is the final example illustrating dynamic behaviour with JavaScript but there is a graphic representation of the Document Object Model (DOM) shown overleaf for further explanation of how the objects in a web page are related.

DOM Hierarchy Reference Chart

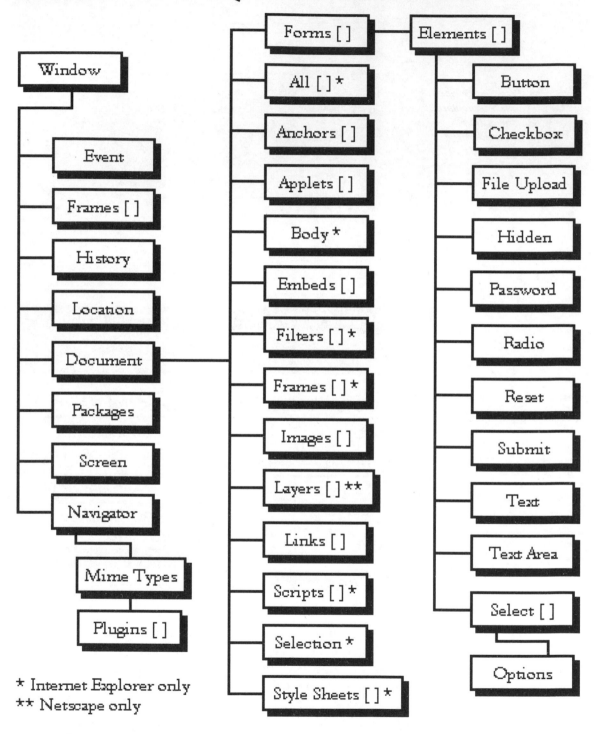

Window

- Event
- Frames [ ]
- History
- Location
- Document
- Packages
- Screen
- Navigator
  - Mime Types
    - Plugins [ ]

Document

- Forms [ ]
- All [ ] *
- Anchors [ ]
- Applets [ ]
- Body *
- Embeds [ ]
- Filters [ ] *
- Frames [ ] *
- Images [ ]
- Layers [ ] **
- Links [ ]
- Scripts [ ] *
- Selection *
- Style Sheets [ ] *

Forms [ ] → Elements [ ]

- Button
- Checkbox
- File Upload
- Hidden
- Password
- Radio
- Reset
- Submit
- Text
- Text Area
- Select [ ]
  - Options

* Internet Explorer only
** Netscape only

JavaScript In E-Commerce

This final chapter shows how some of the earlier examples may be applied to e-commerce applications and illustrates how frames can store data for later use in other frames.

Covers

Chapter Fourteen

Products Page

The example in this chapter follows the development of an on-line order that starts with a page from which the user may select quantities of items to order.

The page is framed with a left-hand panel named "menu" and a right-hand larger frame named "main".

Typically the menu frame will remain constantly displayed while the main frame will display different pages as the user navigates around the site.

A button is added at the bottom of the form that will advance the user to the next stage of the order process.

In the form, depicted below, the user has entered quantity requirement for some of the illustrated products:

Enhance this page with the addition of popup windows over each image giving fuller product details for that item.

Hidden Form

The page in the menu frame contains a hidden form named "m" (for memory) that will retain the order data while the pages in the main frame are changed.

It consists of input items that mirror those of the form named "f" on the product page together with inputs for customer name, account number and order number.

```
<FORM NAME = "m" METHOD = "post"
ACTION = "mailto:shapes@domain.com"
ENCTYPE = "text/plain">
<INPUT TYPE = "hidden" NAME = "customer" VALUE = "">
<INPUT TYPE = "hidden" NAME = "accountnum" VALUE = "">
<INPUT TYPE = "hidden" NAME = "ordernum" VAMUE = "">
<INPUT TYPE = "hidden" NAME = "ball" VALUE = "">
<INPUT TYPE = "hidden" NAME = "hoop" VALUE = "">
<INPUT TYPE = "hidden" NAME = "cone" VALUE = "">
</FORM>
```

The onclick attribute of the button on the products page calls a JavaScript function that fills the values of the hidden form with the values entered by the user into the products page form "f", then loads a new page into the main frame.

The frames must be named with the name attribute of the <frame> tags on the frameholder page.

```
<SCRIPT TYPE= "text/javascript">
<!--
function populate(){

parent.frames.menu.document.m.ball.value =
document.f.ball.value;

parent.frames.menu.document.m.hoop.value =
document.f.hoop.value;

parent.frames.menu.document.m.cone.value =
document.f.cone.value;                }

window.location = "customer.htm";
}
//-->
</SCRIPT>
```

Customer Details

The next page in the main frame requests the customer name and account number which are again added to the memory form "m" in the menu frame by the form button.

```
<SCRIPT TYPE = "text/javascript">
<!--
function populate(){
parent.frames.menu.document.m.customer.value =
document.f.customer.value;
parent.frames.menu.document.m.accountnum.value =
document.f.accountnum.value;
window.location = "confirm.htm";
}
//-->
</SCRIPT>
```

Add validation routines to check that the user has made valid entries.

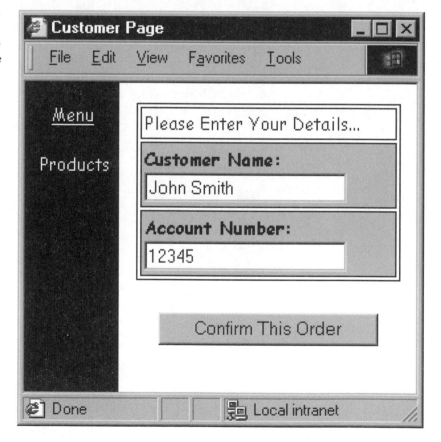

Generate Order Number

The final page that appears in the order process contains all details of the customer's order for the user to confirm before submitting the order form.

These details are dynamically written by JavaScript with data retrieved from the hidden form in the menu frame page.

It is useful to allocate a unique number to the customer's order for identification purposes.

The JavaScript on the confirmation page first generates this number, then stores it in the hidden form in the menu frame.

Typically a date object can provide an order number using parts of the current time concatenated into a single number.

In this script the order number will comprise of the final number in the year followed by the month number, then the hour, minute and second:

It is unlikely but possible that two different customers could generate the same order number at exactly the same time.

```
<SCRIPT TYPE= "text/javascript">
<!--

var d = new Date();
var yr = ( d.getYear() ).toString();
yr = yr.charAt(3);
var mo = ( d.getMonth() ).toString();
var hr = ( d.getHours() ).toString();
var mn = ( d.getMinutes() ).toString();
var sc = (d.getSeconds() ).toString();
var onum = yr + mo + hr + mn + sc;

parent.frames.menu.document.m.ordernum.value = onum;
```

The script continues on the next page to dynamically write page content using data from the hidden form to state the order number, customer name and account number.

Items required on the order and their quantity are then listed only for those items where the user has made an entry.

Confirm Order

```
document.write( "Order No. " +
parent.frames.menu.document.m.ordernum.value );
document.write( "<BR>For " +
parent.frames.menu.document.m.customer.value );
document.write( "<BR>Account No. " +
parent.frames.menu.document.m.accountnum.value );
if( parent.frames.menu.document.m.ball.value != "" )
document.write(parent.frames.menu.document.m.ball.value
+ " Balls @ £7.99 each<BR>" );
if( parent.frames.menu.document.m.hoop.value != "" )
document.write(parent.frames.menu.document.m.hoop.value
+ " Hoops @ £3.99 each<BR>" );
if( parent.frames.menu.document.m.cone.value != "" )
document.write(parent.frames.menu.document.m.cone.value
+ " Cones @ £5.99 each<BR>" );
```

Place the script block in the body of the html document and write the table from JavaScript too.

Submit Order

The JavaScript block on this final page in the order process includes a function to submit the hidden form in the menu frame when the user pushes the form button.

```
function sendorder(){
parent.frames.menu.document.m.submit();
}

//-->
</SCRIPT>
```

Typically the form would be sent to a CGI script on the web server but this form is submitted by e-mail to illustrate the content in plain text form.

Add a feature to navigate back to the order page so the user can amend the order if required.

From: John Smith   To: shapes@domain.com
Subject: Form posted from Microsoft Internet Explorer.

```
customer=John Smith
accountnum=12345
ordernum=0713721
ball=5
hoop=
cone=8
```

Items that have no quantity entered such as the hoop value above contain the empty string that was initially assigned to them in the html code.

These could be replaced using an onsubmit routine to loop through the inputs and replace any empty string values with a zero.

All the order details have now been sent to the supplier and the JavaScript on-line order process is complete.

What Next ?

The future looks bright for JavaScript with the introduction of the SVG file format to display Scalable Vector Graphics.

This file format stores vector graphic information in text form within a XML document.

File sizes of SVG images are very small compared to GIF and JPG images and have the advantage that the image can be scaled-up without increasing file size.

Also most importantly the elements of the image can be manipulated by JavaScript to create animation and interactive effects.

The screenshot showing text, star shape and drop-shadow effect are all written in a text format using the SVG file format.

Learn more about the SVG file format from the W3C website at http://www.w3c.org.

Jasc Software, creators of Paint Shop Pro, have a program called Trajectory Pro that creates vector graphics as SVG images available from their website at http://www.jasc.com.

Adobe Illustrator 9.0 supports SVG images and includes an Interactivity Palette to create dynamic SVG with JavaScript.

Adobe have also created the PC browser plug-in needed to support the SVG format which can be automatically installed on browsers without SVG capability and is freely available at http://www.adobe.com/svg/viewer/install/.

The further extension of the browser DOM together with these exciting developments in SVG should ensure that JavaScript will continue adding magic to future websites.

Index

D

M

N

O